KU-724-501

Contents

A note about copyright

Dear Customer

What does the little © mean and why does it matter?

Your market-leading BPP books, course materials and e-learning materials do not write and update themselves. People write them: on their own behalf or as employees of an organisation that invests in this activity. Copyright law protects their livelihoods. It does so by creating rights over the use of the content.

Breach of copyright is a form of theft – as well being a criminal offence in some jurisdictions, it is potentially a serious breach of professional ethics.

With current technology, things might seem a bit hazy but, basically, without the express permission of BPP Learning Media:

- Photocopying our materials is a breach of copyright

- Scanning, ripcasting or conversion of our digital materials into different file formats, uploading them to facebook or emailing them to your friends is a breach of copyright

You can, of course, sell your books, in the form in which you have bought them – once you have finished with them. (Is this fair to your fellow students? We update for a reason.) But the i-learns are sold on a single user license basis: we do not supply 'unlock' codes to people who have bought them second hand.

And what about outside the UK? BPP Learning Media strives to make our materials available at prices students can afford by local printing arrangements, pricing policies and partnerships which are clearly listed on our website. A tiny minority ignore this and indulge in criminal activity by illegally photocopying our material or supporting organisations that do. If they act illegally and unethically in one area, can you really trust them?

AA

Qualific   )

LEVEL
AAT AC

Workbo

2015 Ed

657 ACCOUNTING : REFERENCE
631790

First edition June 2011
Fifth edition June 2015

ISBN 9781 4727 2211 9

British Library Cataloguing-in-Publication Data
A catalogue record for this book is available from the British Library

Published by
BPP Learning Media Ltd
BPP House
Aldine Place
London
W12 8AA

www.bpp.com/learningmedia

Printed in the United Kingdom by RICOH UK Limited
Unit 2
Wells Place
Merstham
RH1 3LG

Your learning materials, published by BPP Learning Media Ltd, are printed on paper obtained from traceable sustainable sources.

This Workbook for Level 1 has been written specifically to ensure comprehensive yet concise coverage of the assessment criteria. It is fully up to date as at June 2015 and reflects both the AAT's study guide and the sample assessments provided by the AAT.

How to use this Workbook

This workbook contains odd-numbered chapters containing the learning you need to do to prepare yourself for the assessment, and even-numbered chapters giving you assessment practice in the form of assessment style tasks.

You should work through the book taking each chapter in turn, working through the information presented to you and then attempting the tasks given. You can compare your answers with the answers given towards the back of the Workbook. If you have struggled with any tasks, look back at the learning chapter to see where you have gone wrong. At the end of the Workbook there are the two sample assessments provided by the AAT plus two assessment-standard practice assessments prepared by BPP for you to work through. You should not attempt these until you have tried all the tasks in the even-numbered chapters. These sample and practice assessments have answers so that you can judge how you are doing once you have completed them.

If you have any comments about this book, please email nisarahmed@bpp.com or write to Nisar Ahmed, AAT Head of Programme, BPP Learning Media Ltd, BPP House, Aldine Place, London W12 8AA.

Learning outcomes

This assessment relates to four units.

Each of the units has a number of learning outcomes with assessment criteria in which learners will need to demonstrate competence to complete this assessment.

Each chapter in this workbook relates to the learning outcomes and assessment criteria below. Note that even-numbered chapters are assessment practice relating to the preceding chapter.

Essential accounting procedures

The Purpose of the Unit

This unit enables learners to understand and apply basic accounting terminology and procedures.

Learning Objectives

This unit introduces the learner to some basic general accounting procedures.

Learning Outcomes

This unit consists of six learning outcomes, the learner will:

1. Understand basic accounting terminology **[Chapter 1, section 1]**

2. Understand the use of business documents **[Chapter 1, section 2]**

3. Prepare to record business transactions in the books of prime entry **[Chapter 1, section 2]**

4. Understand types of coding and batch control **[Chapter 1, sections 3 and 4]**

5. Be able to prepare documents to process receipts and payments **[Chapter 1, section 2]**

6. Be able to prepare a basic profit statement **[Chapter 1, section 1]**

Delivery guidance

Learners must be able to complete tasks on the topics and procedures specified below.

General

- The learner will **not** be expected to understand or use the double entry bookkeeping system.

- The learner will **not** be expected to understand or calculate VAT but VAT will be shown on invoices and credit notes.

- It is expected that learners are able to use a standard calculator.

Learning outcome 1 – Understand basic accounting terminology

Assessment criteria

1.1 Explain the terms assets, liabilities, income and expenditure. **[Chapter 1, section 1]**

1.2 Identify examples of assets, liabilities, income and expenditure. **[Chapter 1, section 1]**

The learner should be able to explain these terms in their simplest form. The learner will not be expected to provide definitions in accordance with accounting standards. The learner should be able to classify items as assets, liabilities, income or expenditure but will not be asked to differentiate between fixed and current assets or long term and current liabilities.

1.3 Explain the terminology associated with the sale and purchase of goods for cash and on credit. **[Chapter 1, section 1]**

The learner should understand and be able to explain, in basic terms, the meaning of sales, cash sales, credit sales, purchases, cash purchases, credit purchases, customer, supplier, receipt, payment, debtor and creditor.

1.4 Identify examples of cash transactions and credit transactions. **[Chapter 1, section 1]**

The learner should understand that cash transactions involve immediate payment and credit transactions are when payment is delayed. The use of credit cards will not be tested.

1.5 Explain the terms profit and loss. **[Chapter 1, section 1]**

The learner should understand that when income exceeds expenditure there is a profit but if expenditure exceeds income there is a loss. The learner should understand that gross profit is sales less cost of sales and net profit is gross profit less expenses. Learners are not expected to understand the constituent parts of cost of sales. Understanding of cost of sales is limited to the fact that cost of sales are the cost to the business of the items sold.

Learning outcome 2 – Understand the use of business documents

Assessment criteria

2.1 Identify documents used in the process of buying and selling goods on credit and when they are used. **[Chapter 1, section 2]**

2.2 Identify documents used to process cash sales and cash purchases. **[Chapter 1, section 2]**

The learner should recognise and understand the use of invoices, credit notes, a purchases order, a statement of account, a remittance advice and receipts. The learner will not be asked to prepare any of these documents but they are expected to understand the information contained in each.

BPP
LEARNING MEDIA

Learning outcome 3 – Prepare to record business transactions in the books of prime entry

Assessment criteria

3.1 Select appropriate documents to record transactions in the books of prime entry. **[Chapter 1, section 3]**

3.2 Select the appropriate book of prime entry to record transactions relating to credit sales and credit purchases. **[Chapter 1, section 3]**

3.3 Select the appropriate book of prime entry to record payments made and monies received. **[Chapter 1, section 3]**

The learner should recognise invoices (sales and purchase) and credit notes and understand that they are entered as appropriate into the sales, purchases or returns day books. The learner should recognise cheques, paying in slips, cheques paid and received listings, cash paid and received listings and understand that they are entered as appropriate into the cash receipts or cash payments book. The learner should be able to match a document to the appropriate book of prime entry. The learner will not be required to make entries into the books of prime entry.

Learning outcome 4 – Understand types of coding and batch control

Assessment criteria

4.1 Identify types of codes used when recording financial transactions. **[Chapter 1, section 4]**

The learner should understand the difference between numerical codes, alphabetical codes and alphanumerical codes.

4.2 Explain what is meant by a batch control system. **[Chapter 1, section 3]**

The learner should be aware that purchases and sales invoices and credit notes can be entered in the accounting system individually or in batches as a time saving measure.

Learning outcome 5 – Be able to prepare documents to process receipts and payments

Assessment criteria

5.1 Complete a bank paying-in slip for notes, coins and cheques. **[Chapter 1, section 2]**

The learner should be able to enter notes, coins and cheques for banking on the front of a paying in slip. The learner should be able to total the amounts as required. The learner should also be aware of the need to sign and date the paying in slip.

5.2 Complete a cheque. **[Chapter 1, section 2]**

The learner should be able to prepare a cheque ready for an authorised signature. The learner should be aware of the need for the words and figures to match. The learner must be able to date the cheque in full and understand the need for the date to be correct. Learners should be able to insert the name of the payee and understand that the payee is the person or business to whom the amount on the cheque is being paid.

Learning outcome 6 – Be able to prepare a basic profit statement

Assessment criteria

6.1 Calculate gross profit. **[Chapter 1, section 1]**

6.2 Calculate net profit. **[Chapter 1, section 1]**

The learner should be able to calculate gross profit from sales and cost of sales figures. The learner should be able to total up to five expense figures and deduct the result from gross profit to arrive at net profit.

Mathematics for accounting

The purpose of the unit

Learners should be able to perform a range of basic mathematical functions using financial data.

Learning objectives

This unit is about gaining a range of numerical skills required by a financial professional.

Learning outcome

This unit consists of one learning outcome; the learner will be able to apply basic mathematical concepts to financial data. **[Chapter 3, sections 2 to 8]**

Delivery guidance

Learners must be able to complete tasks on the topics and procedures specified below.

General

It is expected that learners are able to use a standard calculator.

Learning outcome – Be able to apply basic mathematical concepts to financial data

Assessment criteria

1.1 Add and subtract whole numbers and numbers up to two decimal places. **[Chapter 3, section 2]**

The learner should be able to add and subtract up to five numbers which may be a mixture of whole numbers, numbers to one decimal place and numbers to two decimal places.

1.2 Multiply and divide whole numbers and numbers up to two decimal places. **[Chapter 3, section 3]**

The learner should be able to multiply and divide any two numbers which may be a mixture of whole numbers, numbers to one decimal place and numbers to two decimal places.

1.3 Calculate the ratio or proportion of two numbers. **[Chapter 3, sections 4 and 5]**

The learner should be able to calculate the ratio or proportion of one whole number to another whole number. The resultant answer can be a fraction, for example ½, or a ratio. In the case of a ratio the answer will always be in the format of one number to a base figure of one, for example 3:1.

1.4 Calculate the percentage of one number in relation to another number. **[Chapter 3, section 6]**

The learner should be able to calculate what percentage one whole number is of another whole number. The resultant answer may be a whole number, a number to one decimal place or a number to two decimal places.

1.5 Find a percentage of a whole number. **[Chapter 3, section 6]**

Learners should be able to calculate a given percentage figure of a whole number. The resultant answer may be a whole number, a number to one decimal place or a number to two decimal places.

1.6 Apply a fraction to whole numbers. **[Chapter 3, section 7]**

Learners should be able to calculate a given fraction of a whole number. The resultant answer may be a whole number, a number to one decimal place or a number to two decimal places.

1.7 Calculate the average of a range of numbers. **[Chapter 3, section 8]**

Learners should be able to calculate the average value of a range of up to five numbers. The resultant answer may be a whole number, a number to one decimal place or a number to two decimal places.

Accounting in a professional environment

The purpose of the unit

Learners will be able to understand the role of a finance professional in any organisation and apply ethical behaviour and professionalism within an accounting environment.

Learning objectives

This unit is about gaining a range of transferable skills with regard to working practices and appropriate behaviours expected of a finance professional.

Learning outcomes

This unit consists of four learning outcomes, the learner will:

1. Understand basic organisations and how the finance professional contributes to the organisation **[Chapter 5, sections 1 and 2]**

2. Understand the need to apply appropriate ethical behaviour and professionalism within an accounting environment **[Chapter 5, sections 3 to 5]**

3. Understand that there is a legal framework within which organisations must operate **[Chapter 5, sections 3 and 6]**

4. Understand how efficient working practices and personal development contribute to achievement **[Chapter 5, sections 7 to 9]**

Delivery guidance

Learners must be able to complete tasks on the topics and procedures specified below.

Learning outcome 1 – Understand basic organisations and how the finance professional contributes to the organisation

Assessment criteria

1.1 Identify different types of business organisation. **[Chapter 5, section 1]**

The learner should be aware of the different types of organisation in the private sector (limited companies, partnerships and sole traders), public sector (councils, NHS, Police, Fire and Ambulance Services) and also Charitable organisations. Knowledge of these organisations is limited to knowing which sector different types of organisation fall into. Learners should understand that organisations in the private sector exist to make a profit as compared to those in the public and charitable sectors where profit is not a primary purpose.

1.2 Identify the 'customers' of the accounting function. **[Chapter 5, section 2]**

The learner should understand that any user of information produced by the finance function could be considered to be a customer of the service. The learner should appreciate that it is important to meet the needs of the 'customer' in order that the information provided by the finance professional is fit for purpose. Learners'

understanding of the term 'customers' should be restricted to other departments within the organisation, suppliers and trade customers.

1.3 Explain how the accounting function can support an organisation. **[Chapter 5, section 2]**

The learner should understand that the finance function produces information which enables managers to run the organisation effectively and efficiently. The types of information learners are expected to understand is limited to information about whether a business is making a profit or loss, information about actual income and expenditure and how it compares with what the business had planned. The importance of complete, accurate and timely information should be appreciated.

Learning outcome 2 – Understand the need to apply appropriate ethical behaviour and professionalism within an accounting environment

Assessment criteria

2.1 Explain how to maintain confidentiality of information. **[Chapter 5, section 3]**

The learner should be able to understand that financial information is sensitive and why the information should be kept confidential. They are expected to identify ways of keeping information confidential. Examples include, but are not restricted to, ensuring all documents are in secure storage and not left on desks or in unlocked cupboards as well as ensuring information stored electronically is password protected and not left visible on unattended workstations.

2.2 Explain the importance of ethical and professional behaviour to the role of those in the accounting function. **[Chapter 5, section 4]**

The learner should understand the meaning of ethics in the context of the role of a finance professional, with particular reference to the importance of having up to date technical knowledge and acting with honesty and integrity. Learners will not be expected to provide an explanation of any of the fundamental principles of professional ethics.

2.3 Identify the importance of an organisation adopting environmentally and socially responsible policies. **[Chapter 5, section 5]**

The learner should understand that the behaviour of organisations will impact upon the environment. Examples include but are not restricted to organisations having paper saving and fuel saving policies to reduce the negative environmental impact of an organisation.

Learning outcome 3 – Understand that there is a legal framework within which organisations must operate

Assessment criteria

3.1 Identify the responsibility an organisation has to the health and safety of its employees and of visitors to its premises. **[Chapter 5, section 6]**

Learners should know that organisations have a duty of care to all employees, customers, visitors and anyone on their premises. Learners also need to know that the employee has a duty to behave in a safe manner to ensure they do not put themselves or colleagues in danger. The learner does not need to know any specific legislative details or the content of the statute.

3.2 Explain the role of an employee in the accounting function in maintaining safe and effective working practices. **[Chapter 5, section 6]**

The learner should understand that if they see unsafe practice they have a duty to report it to a superior. They should understand the importance of keeping a tidy work area both in respect of safety but also in respect of efficient working practice.

3.3 Identify how an employee in the accounting function can ensure that personal information is protected and not disclosed without authority. **[Chapter 5, section 3]**

Learners must understand why personal information cannot be passed to unauthorised people. They should understand that paper based information should be stored securely and not left on desks or in unlocked cupboards. In addition when the information is stored electronically the computer should be locked when the employee is away from their workstation and sensitive files should be password protected.

Learning outcome 4 – Understand how efficient working practices and personal development contribute to achievement

Assessment criteria

4.1 Identify efficient working practices which contribute to the achievement of own and team goals. **[Chapter 5, section 7]**

The learner should understand that working as a team will achieve far more than each individual working independently. They should appreciate that during busy times individuals within a department/team should help each other in order to complete tasks within deadlines. Learners should understand that they ought to have some form of work plan to help analyse work tasks and ensure they are achieved on time. Examples include, but are not restricted to, a 'to do' list, an in tray, a diary and a schedule.

4.2 Explain how communication within the team contributes to its overall efficiency. [Chapter 5, section 7]

The learner should understand that an individual within a team does not work in isolation and there are others within the team who are relying on information produced by the individual in order to complete their work within deadlines. Consequently when individual deadlines are not going to be met there must be communication with others affected by this in order that contingency planning can take place. Similarly this applies to teams within an organisation.

4.3 Identify the personal skills required to work in the accounting function. [Chapter 5, section 8]

The learner should be able to identify the skills, attributes and behaviours required of someone working in an accounting environment. These include (but are not restricted to) being reliable, numerate, punctual, showing willingness to learn, having good communication skills and being honest, straightforward and organised.

4.4 Identify ways in which new skills and knowledge can be acquired. [Chapter 5, section 8]

The learner should understand that formal training is a way of acquiring new skills and knowledge but there are other ways of acquiring knowledge and skills. These include self study of professional journals, books and the internet, job rotation, on the job training and job shadowing.

4.5 Explain how the acquisition of new skills can be agreed and subsequently reviewed with the line manager. [Chapter 5, section 9]

Learners should understand that having a mentor/manager who works closely with them to support their development is beneficial. They should understand that the acquisition of new skills should be discussed and agreed prior to acquiring the skills and afterwards there should be a process of review and evaluation to gain the maximum benefit from such development opportunities.

Creating business documents

The purpose of the unit

This unit introduces learners to a range of business documents used within the accounting function and other areas of a business.

Learning objectives

This unit introduces the learner to the importance of good quality communication by raising awareness of the documents used by a business for formal and informal written communication, both within and outside the business.

Learning outcomes

This unit consists of three learning outcomes, the learner will:

1. Know that there are different types of business documents
   [Chapter 7, sections 1 and 2]

2. Know why it is important to use the right communication style in business
   documents **[Chapter 7, sections 2 and 3]**

3. Be able to produce routine business documents **[Chapter 7, section 3]**

Delivery guidance

Learners must be able to complete tasks on the topics and procedures specified below.

Learning outcome 1 – Know that there are different types of business document

Assessment criteria

1.1 Identify different types of business document and when they might be used.
[Chapter 7, section 1]

The learner should be able to identify letters, emails, memos and reports and
understand the circumstances in which each document is used as an appropriate
form of communication. Learners should understand that some other business
documents are also a form of communication.

These include, but are not restricted to, sales invoices, purchase invoices, credit
notes, statements of account and remittance advices.

1.2 State why templates are used for some business documents. **[Chapter 7, section 2]**

The learner should understand the reason why organisations use templates. The
learner should understand that consistency of documentation is important both
within the organisation but also in presenting a consistent, positive message to
customers which also supports the organisation's core goals and ethos.

Learning outcome 2 – Know why it is important to use the right communication style in business documents

Assessment criteria

2.1 State why some businesses adopt a 'house style' for certain documents.
[Chapter 7, section 2]

The learner should understand the reason why organisations adopt house styles.
The learner should understand that consistency of documentation is important both
within the organisation but also in presenting a consistent, positive message to
customers which also supports the organisation's core goals and ethos.

BPP
LEARNING MEDIA

2.2 Give examples of when to use a formal or informal communication style. [Chapter 7, section 3]

The learner should understand that communications to stakeholders (including customers and suppliers) must present a positive, professional image. The importance of communicating using acceptable business English and not using slang, text or other abbreviated language should be clearly understood by learners. They must be able to decide when it is appropriate to communicate in a formal manner and when it is more effective to use an informal communication style, for example when to send a letter and when to send an email.

Learning outcome 3 – Be able to produce routine business documents

Assessment criteria

3.1 Produce routine business documents using the appropriate communication style. [Chapter 7, section 3]

3.2 Check documents for accuracy. [Chapter 7, section 3]

The learner should be able to structure and select appropriate content for inclusion in letters, memos, emails and reports. Learners should understand that letters must be dated, addressed to the recipient, include a suitable heading and a greeting with an appropriate salutation. Learners should be aware that memos, emails and reports must be dated, show who they are 'To' and 'From' and show the subject matter. Learners should understand that all of these forms of communication should contain an introduction followed by the main content and finally a short sentence or two in conclusion. Learners will not be expected to differentiate between formal and informal reports.

Learners should be able to check letters, emails and memos and identify any errors.

Assessment summary

Assessment name AAT Access – Level 1 Award in accounting

Level 1 Duration One and a half hours (90 minutes)

Competency For the purpose of assessment the competency level for AAT assessment is set at 70 per cent. The level descriptor below describes the ability and skills students at this level must successfully demonstrate to achieve competence.

QCF Level descriptor Summary

Achievement at Level 1 reflects the ability to use relevant knowledge, skills and procedures to complete routine tasks. It includes responsibility for completing tasks and procedures subject to direction or guidance.

Knowledge and understanding

- Use knowledge of facts, procedures and ideas to complete well defined, routine tasks.
- Be aware of information relevant to the area of study or work.

Application and action

- Complete well defined routine tasks.
- Use relevant skills and procedures.
- Select and use relevant information.
- Identify whether actions have been effective.

Autonomy and accountability

- Take responsibility for completing tasks and procedures subject to direction or guidance as needed.

The purpose of the assessment is to allow the learner to demonstrate skills and knowledge commensurate with the accounting and business environment at Level 1.

The assessment should not present any surprises to well prepared students. Please read this guidance in conjunction with the standards for the unit.

The assessment is designed to allow the learners to perform a series of short tasks that cover basic business Maths and English, communication skills and knowledge of the accounting environment and related procedures. The assessment consists of 22 tasks – 12 in section one and 10 in section two. The learner must prove competence in each section to be successful.

1

Essential accounting procedures

Chapter coverage

This chapter covers the unit Essential Accounting Procedures and therefore introduces the essential accounting procedures you need to understand for your assessment.

1 Terminology

Organisations exist to do something, usually this is providing goods or services, often to make a profit. In doing this many organisations buy and sell things (carry out transactions). If they buy things, they may own things (assets).

Organisation A — buys a building → Organisation A owns a building

Sometimes, in order to buy something, organisations need to borrow money. If they borrow, they owe other parties money (have liabilities).

Organisation A borrows from the bank to buy a building money → Organisation A owes the bank

> **KEYWORDS**
>
> An **asset** is something the organisation owns.
>
> A **liability** is something the organisation owes.
>
> **Expenditure** is when the organisation spends to purchase goods or services for the organisation or to resell.
>
> **Income** is what the organisation earns when it makes sales of goods or services to other parties.

You need to learn these definitions. Knowing what these terms mean is crucial in your assessment.

How it works

The following are examples of assets, liabilities, expenditure and income.

Item	Classification	Further definition
Premises	Asset	The building the organisation operates from.
Motor vehicles	Asset	The vehicles the organisation uses.
Plant/equipment	Asset	The machines the organisation uses to operate.
Inventory (stock)	Asset	The goods produced or bought for resale by the organisation.
Bank account	Asset (but see overdraft below)	The cash owned by an organisation.
Overdraft	Liability	The cash owed to the bank by the organisation if it has a negative (red) balance with the bank.
Bank loan	Liability	The amount owed by an organisation to the bank if the bank has lent it money for any reason.
Other loan	Liability	Other parties may lend money to a organisation, in which case the organisation owes them money.
Sales	Income	Earnings resulting from selling items to customers.
Bank interest received	Income	Earnings resulting from having money saved in the bank.
Purchases (raw materials or goods for resale)	Expenditure	Expenditure on items to produce or sell to customers.

Item	Classification	Further definition
Payments to staff	Expenditure	Wages and salaries paid to staff working in the business.
Insurance	Expenditure	Payments to insure assets against loss or damage.
Advertising	Expenditure	Payments made to advertise an organisation's products.
Road tax/fuel/motor expenses	Expenditure	Payments made to use the organisation's vehicles.

Note about expenditure – there could be a large number of examples of different services an organisation spends money on. Only a small number have been given here to illustrate – try to think of some more in an organisation with which you are familiar.

TASK 1 **Place the items listed below into the appropriate box.**

Premises, advertising cost, sale, bank loan, insurance, fuel costs, interest received, inventory, bank overdraft, salaries

Assets	Liabilities

Income	Expenditure

Credit transactions

Liabilities are made when an organisation borrows, or does not pay immediately for something it has bought. An organisation may not pay for its purchases straightaway because it has been extended **credit** by another organisation.

KEYWORDS

A **customer** is a person who buys goods or services.

A **supplier** is a person who sells goods and services to a customer.

A **cash sale** is a transaction to sell goods or services when payment is made immediately.

A **credit sale** is a transaction to sell goods or services when payment is made at a later date than the delivery or goods or provision of the service.

A **cash purchase** is a transaction to purchase goods or services when payment is made immediately.

A **credit purchase** is a transaction to purchase goods or services when payment is made at a later date than the delivery of goods or provision of the service.

A **debtor** or **receivable** is an asset. It is the amount that a customer owes to the organisation (who is its supplier) at a later date in respect of a credit sale.

A **creditor** or **payable** is a liability. It is the amount the organisation (as a customer) owes a supplier to be paid at a later date in respect of a credit purchase.

How it works

Paper Products is an organisation which makes printed boxes and other items. It has a customer, Applebys, and a supplier, Pearmans. It has **credit** transactions with both of them.

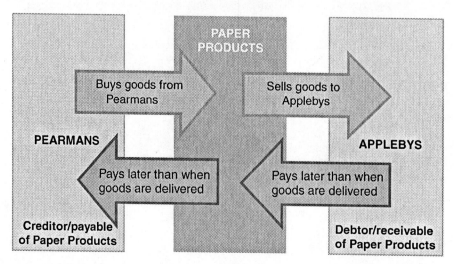

Wood Works is an organisation which makes wooden items. It has a customer, Cherryton, and a supplier, Banarama. It has **cash** transactions with both of them.

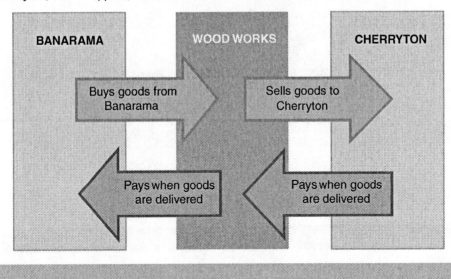

TASK 2   **Place the items listed below into the appropriate box.**

Sale of goods when payment is made at a date later than delivery
Sale of goods when cash is paid on delivery
Sale of services when cash is paid at a date later than the service was provided
Sale of services when cash is paid on delivery of the service
Purchase of goods when payment is made at the same time as delivery of the goods
Purchase of services when payment is made at the same time as the service is provided
Purchase of goods when payment is made at a date later than delivery
Purchase of a service when payment is made at a later date than the service is provided

Cash sale	Credit sale
Cash purchase	Credit purchase

How much an organisation spends and how much it sells at a given price level determines whether it is successful, and able to continue in business.

> ### KEYWORDS
>
> Profit is what an organisation makes if income is greater than expenditure in a financial period.
>
> A loss is what an organisation makes if income is less than expenditure in a financial period.

How it works

Organisation A	
	£
Income	100,000
Expenditure	80,000
Profit	20,000

Organisation B	
	£
Income	50,000
Expenditure	75,000
Loss	(25,000)

In these examples:

Organisation A has **spent £20,000 less than** it **earned** in the financial period. This is therefore a **profit** for that period.

Organisation B has **spent £25,000 more than** it **earned** in the financial period. This is therefore a **loss** for that period.

Note that expenditure is sometimes shown in brackets to show that it is being subtracted from income.

A loss is often shown in brackets to show that it is a negative number, rather than being shown as –£25,000.

Often in financial information, profit is divided into different elements so that users can see the impact of different parts of an organisation's expenditure.

KEYWORDS

Gross profit is income less direct cost of sales.

Cost of sales is the cost to the organisation of the items sold.

Net profit is gross profit less other expenses.

In other words, the total expenditure is divided up into two kinds of expenditure: direct cost of sales, and other expenditure (expenses).

How it works

Organisation A		Organisation A's total expenditure	
	£		
Income	100,000		
Cost of sales	40,000	→	40,000
Gross profit	60,000		
Expenses	40,000	→	40,000
Net profit	20,000		80,000

TASK 3 Profit and loss

1   The balance of an organisation's income and expenditure results in profit or loss.

Which ONE of the following statements is true?

When income exceeds profit, an organisation has made a loss ☐

When income exceeds expenditure, an organisation has made a profit ☐

When income exceeds expenditure, an organisation has made a loss ☐

2   The balance of an organisation's income and expenditure results in profit or loss.

Which ONE of the following statements is true?

When expenditure exceeds profit, an organisation has made a loss ☐

When expenditure exceeds income, an organisation has made a profit ☐

When expenditure exceeds income, an organisation has made a loss ☐

3   Profit is classified as gross profit or net profit.

Which ONE of the following statements is untrue?

Income less total expenditure equals net profit   ☐

Income less cost of sales equals gross profit   ☐

Income less expenses only equals net profit   ☐

4   Profit is classified as gross profit or net profit.

Which ONE of the following statements is untrue?

Gross profit less expenses equals net profit   ☐

Cost of sales plus expenses equals total expenditure   ☐

Income less cost of sales equals net profit   ☐

5   **Using the information in the first two tables, place a tick in the appropriate column of the third table below to show whether each of the organisations has made a profit or a loss. You should not place more than one tick (✓) against each organisation.**

Organisation A	
	£
Income	80,000
Expenditure	70,000

Organisation B	
	£
Income	150,000
Expenditure	120,000

Organisation	Profit	Loss
Organisation A		
Organisation B		

You must be able to calculate gross profit and net profit. This means that you must:

(1)   Remember what makes up both gross profit and net profit
(2)   Do the calculation

The best way to be able to do these calculations is to practise them over and over again. There are questions for you to practise in the next chapter and the practice assessments at the end of the Workbook, but you should also run through the following practice questions in Task 4.

TASK 4

Organisation A	
	£
Income	120,000
Cost of sales	45,000
Expenses	45,000

Organisation B	
	£
Income	364,600
Cost of sales	149,400
Expenses	55,780

1   Calculate gross profit for Organisation A and Organisation B
2   Calculate net profit for Organisation A and Organisation B

2 Documents

In section 1 we discussed how and when trading organisations buy and sell (transact). Organisations usually provide documents to accompany transactions.

Documents used in credit sales

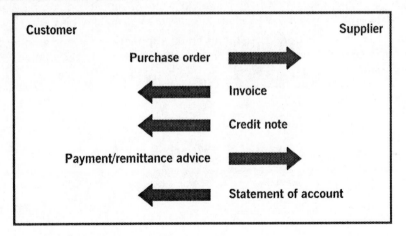

Documents used in cash sales

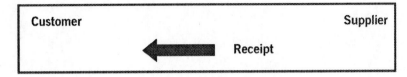

> ### KEYWORDS
>
> An **invoice** is the document a supplier gives a customer when it makes a credit sale to the customer. It shows the customer what amount it owes and when that debt is due to be paid.
>
> A **credit note** is the document a supplier gives a customer when a customer returns items sold on credit. It confirms what goods have been returned, and how much money has been refunded or no longer needs to be paid.
>
> A **purchase order** is the document a customer gives to a supplier requesting that the supplier sells the organisation the goods stated on the order.
>
> A **statement of account** is the document a supplier sends to a customer who it has made credit sales to. It shows the total balance the customer owes to the supplier. In other words, it is a list of invoices that have not yet been paid.
>
> A **remittance advice** is the document a customer sends to a supplier when paying some of its balance with the supplier, so that the supplier can see exactly which invoices are being paid in that payment.
>
> A **receipt** is the document given to a customer for a cash sale, showing the amount of money the customer paid, and what it related to. You are almost certainly familiar with receipts, as you are given one by a shop every time you go shopping.
>
> **NOTE: An organisation is both a customer and a supplier – so, for example, it will send remittance advices to its own suppliers, as well as receiving them from its customers.**

How it works

Here are examples of all the documents listed above

Supplier

Invoice date

Customer

Items being sold

Tax

INVOICE	Invoice number 56314		
Haywood Distributors **Industrial Estate** **Haywood HY4 2SK** **Tel: 01234 563939**			
VAT registration:	0274 2694 49		
Date/tax point:	7 September 20XX		
Order number:	32011		
Customer:	Freeway Superstores 28 Liberty Park Haywood HY4 5TR		
Account number (customer code)	HD 35		
Description/product code	**Quantity**	**Unit amount** **£**	**Total** **£**
Sondy Flat Screen TVs /3200IST25	6	300.00	1,800.00
Net total			1,800.00
VAT at 20%			360.00
Invoice total			2,160.00
Terms 30 days net			

Period after which payment is due

CREDIT NOTE			Credit note number 08641
Haywood Distributors **Industrial Estate** **Haywood HY4 2SK** **Tel: 01234 563939**			
VAT registration:	0274 2694 49		
Date/tax point:	12 September 20XX		
Invoice number:	56314		
Customer:	Freeway Superstores 28 Liberty Park Haywood HY4 5TR		
Account number (customer code)	HD 35		
Description/product code	**Quantity**	**Unit amount** **£**	**Total** **£**
Sondy Flat Screen TVs /3200IST25 Reason for credit note: Delivered damaged	1	300.00	300.00
Net total			300.00
VAT at 20%			60.00
Credit note total			360.00

Items being sold previously and reason for credit

ORDER

Customer

FREEWAY SUPERSTORES
28 Liberty Park
Haywood HY4 5TR
Tel 0303446 Fax 0303447

To: Haywood Distributors
Industrial Estate
Haywood
HY4 2SK

Number: 32011

Date: 5 Sept 20XX

Delivery address: Freeway Superstores
28 Liberty Park
Haywood HY4 5TR

Product code	Quantity	Description	Unit list price £
4425	6	Sondy Flat Screen TVs	300 (excluding VAT)

Items to be bought

Authorised by: *P. Winterbottom*   **Date:** *5 Sept 20XX*

STATEMENT OF ACCOUNT				
Haywood Distributors Industrial Estate Haywood HY4 2SK Tel: 01234 563939 *Supplier*				
VAT registration:	0274 2694 49			
Date:	30 September 20XX			
Customer:	Freeway Superstores 28 Liberty Park Haywood HY4 5TR *Customer*			
Account number (customer code)	HD 35			

Date	Details	Debit £	Credit £	Balance £
21.08.XX	Inv56019	316.40		316.40
28.08.XX	CN08613		47.46	268.94
07.09.XX	Inv56314	2,160.00		2,428.94
12.09.XX	CN08641		360.00	2,068.94
20.09.XX	Payment received – thank you		268.94	1,800.00
Amount now due				1,800.00

Transactions on the credit account – invoices, credit notes and payments

Amount owed at date of statement

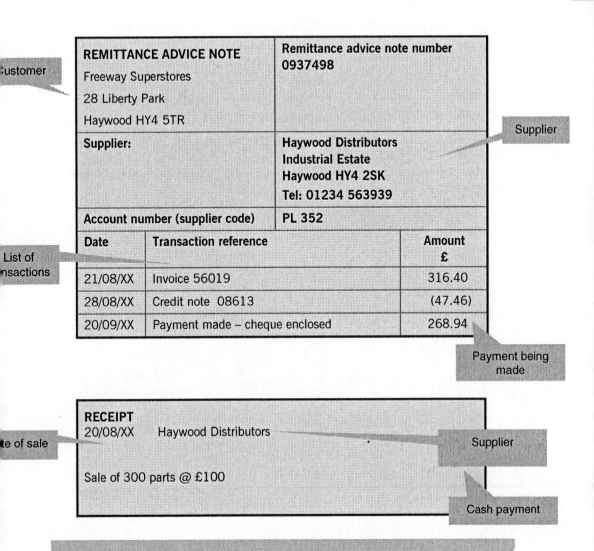

Payment for cash and credit transactions

As outlined above, in organisations payment may be made at the time the goods are traded, for example, when buying a newspaper (a **cash** transaction). Other transactions, particularly those between organisations, are made on credit where the selling organisation allows its customers to pay later (a **credit** transaction).

Ultimately, both types of transaction may be settled in physical cash or by cheque. Paying by cheque results in a slightly more complicated banking procedure than paying in physical cash.

How it works

The customer writes a cheque and gives or sends it to the supplier. The supplier gives the cheque to the bank, which draws money from the customer's bank account as a result and places that money in the supplier's bank account.

Although there is a delay in the cash reaching the supplier's bank account, a cheque payment at the time of exchange of goods is known as a cash transaction. A cheque is considered to be the same as cash. It is the timing of the payment of the cash or the cheque which is important.

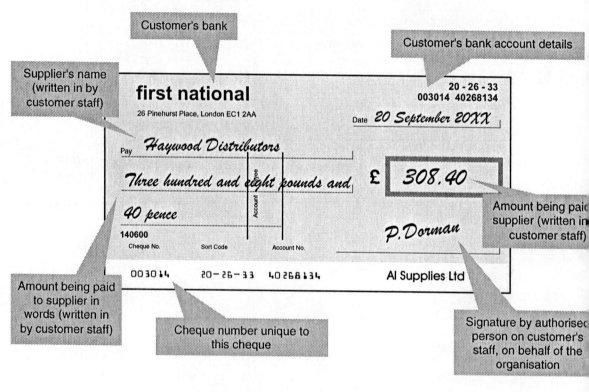

As stated above, when suppliers receive cheques, they must pay them in to the bank. Cash payments may be paid into the bank too. A paying in slip is used when money is paid in to the bank.

How it works

£50 notes by amount
(ie 2 × £50 notes)

Date: 16.3.XX	Date:	MIDWEST BANK	£50 notes	£100.00
A/C 3958229	24 September 20XX		£20 notes	£40.00
			£10 notes	
Cash: £145.00		Account name	£5 notes	£5.00
		Haywood Distributors	£2 coins	
Cheques, POs			£1 coins	
£308.40		Paid in by	Other coin	
Total: £453.40		A Student	Total cash	£145.00
		26-33-20	Cheques, POs	£308.40
000894		3958229	Total £	£453.40

Cheque being paid in

Paying in slip number, unique to this paying in slip

Section retained by company

Section given to the bank

Account details

You are required to know how to fill in a cheque and a paying in slip. Key things to remember are:

(1) Use full names and dates.

(2) On a cheque, write out the amount in words and in numbers in the relevant sections.

(3) On a paying in slip, total cash by note/coin, so for example, 2 × £50 notes is £100, write £100 in the appropriate place.

The best way to learn this skill is to practise it. Try Task 5.

TASK 5 On 21 August 20XX you have been asked to pay the following items into Haywood
Distributors' bank account.

Three	£50 notes
Six	£20 notes
Two	£10 notes
Two	£5 notes
Twenty	50 pence coins
Twelve	20 pence coins
Six	5 pence coins
Two	2 pence coins
Cheque	£253.89

(a) **Complete the paying-in slip below**

Date:	Date:	MIDWEST	£50 notes	
A/C		BANK	£20 notes	
			£10 notes	
Cash:		Account name	£5 notes	
			£2 coins	
Cheques, POs			£1 coins	
		Paid in by	Other coin	
Total:			Total cash	
		26-33-20	Cheques, POs	
006924		3958229	Total £	

On 21 August 20XX you have also been asked to prepare a cheque to send to
Haywood Distributors' supplier, Allison Traders. The payment amount is £506.33.

(b) **Complete the cheque below**

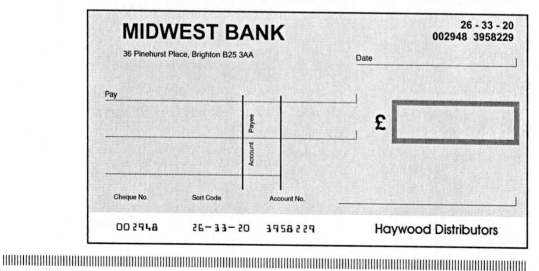

3 Books of prime entry

When an organisation receives documents relating to sales or purchases (cash or credit) it records them in books of prime entry. These are simply the initial records recording certain types of transaction.

How it works

Transaction document received  Details entered into book of prime entry

The key books of prime entry for your purposes are:

Documents you have been introduced to

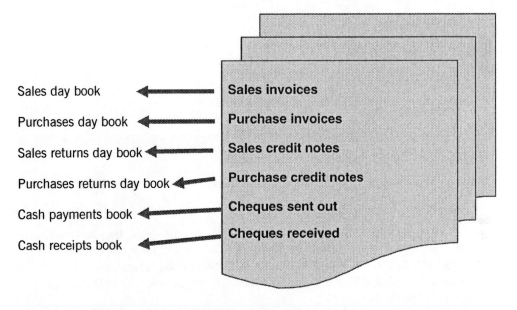

Book of prime entry	Document
Sales day book	Sales invoices
Purchases day book	Purchase invoices
Sales returns day book	Sales credit notes
Purchases returns day book	Purchase credit notes
Cash payments book	Cheques sent out
Cash receipts book	Cheques received

You do not need to know anything more about books of prime entry in your assessment other than which documents are entered into each book. Every time you come across a document in this Workbook, think to yourself, which book of prime entry does this go into? This will help prepare you for such a task in the assessment.

Batching

An organisation can receive a great number of documents in a day. It would take an employee in the accounts department a great deal of time to enter each document separately into the accounts system.

Instead, it is possible to group documents together in a batch, and process them that way. Documents should be batched in like groups (that is, purchase invoices in one batch, sales credit notes in another).

TASK 6 1 **Which of the following documents is entered into the sales day book?**

Purchase invoice   ☐

Cheque received   ☐

Cheque sent out   ☐

Sales invoice   ☐

2 **An organisation will enter a cheque sent to a supplier into which of the following day books?**

Sales day book   ☐

Purchases day book   ☐

Cash payments book   ☐

Cash receipts book   ☐

4 Codes

Look back at the documents you were shown above. In many cases, they had codes on them. Some codes were unique to the document. Some codes were unique to the customer or supplier. Codes help organisations to manage the vast numbers of documents they deal with in the course of business, and be able to refer to specific documents quickly and easily.

There are three main types of code, two of which were shown on the above documents.

KEYWORDS

A numerical code is a code consisting of numbers only.

An alphabetical code is a code consisting of letters only.

An alphanumerical code is a code consisting of numbers and letters, in any order.

How it works

An example of a numerical code is: 00295824

An example of an alphabetical code is: ABCGEDD

An example of an alphanumerical code is: AB2942

Numerical codes usually follow sequentially, so a company might start with its first sales invoice as 00001, then 00002, 00003, 00004 etc. The same might be true of an alphanumerical sequence, for example, if a company coded their invoices SI0001, SI0002, SI0003 and so on.

Customer codes might be alphanumerical, and consist of a combination of the first letters of their name and then a number depending on whether other customers also had those initials. So for example, Northfield Plumbing might be NP001, and another customer, Northern Pumps Ltd, might be NP002.

All you need to know about codes is which type they are and to be able to identify them.

 Look back to the documents given in section 2 and identify the codes on them, noting what type of code each is.

Chapter overview

Organisations usually exist to do something. Many organisations buy and sell things. If they buy things, they may own things (assets).

Sometimes, in order to buy something, organisations need to borrow money. If they borrow, they owe others that money (have liabilities).

You must learn the definitions of assets, liabilities, expenditure and income, profit, loss, gross profit and net profit (see list of keywords) and understand them well enough to do simple calculations of gross profit and net profit.

Organisations make both cash and credit transactions. A credit transaction is when payment is delayed over a prearranged period.

An organisation will send and receive a large number of documents relating to its transactions. The key documents are:

- Invoices
- Credit notes
- Purchase orders
- Statements of account
- Remittance advices
- Receipts

Payments may be made in cash or by cheque. Money will be banked using a paying in slip. You must be able to fill in such documents appropriately.

When a transaction occurs, an organisation will record the details from the initial document into books of prime entry. The books of prime entry are:

- Sales day book
- Purchases day book
- Sales returns day book
- Purchases returns day book
- Cash payments book
- Cash receipts book

You must know which documents are recorded in which books of prime entry.

In order to process large numbers of documents quickly, an organisation may batch documents into groups and process them together.

Organisations use codes to distinguish individual documents. Codes can be numerical, alphabetical and alphanumerical.

Keywords

An **ASSET** is something the organisation owns.

A **LIABILITY** is something the organisation owes.

EXPENDITURE is when the organisation spends to purchase goods or services for the organisation.

INCOME is what the organisation earns when it makes sales of goods or services to other parties.

A **CUSTOMER** is a person who buys goods or services.

A **SUPPLIER** is a person who sells goods and services to a customer.

A **CASH SALE** is a transaction to sell goods or services when payment is made immediately.

A **CREDIT SALE** is a transaction to sell goods or services when payment is made at a later date than the delivery or goods or provision of the service.

A **CASH PURCHASE** is a transaction to purchase goods or services when payment is made immediately.

A **CREDIT PURCHASE** is a transaction to purchase goods or services when payment is made at a later date than the delivery of goods or provision of the service.

A **DEBTOR** or **RECEIVABLE** is an asset. It is the amount that a customer owes to the organisation at a later date in respect of a credit sale.

A **CREDITOR** or **PAYABLE** is a liability. It is the amount the organisation owes a supplier to be paid at a later date in respect of a credit purchase.

PROFIT is what an organisation makes if income is greater than expenditure in a financial period.

A **LOSS** is what an organisation makes if income is less than expenditure in a financial period.

GROSS PROFIT is income less direct cost of sales.

COST OF SALES is the cost to the organisation of the items sold.

NET PROFIT is gross profit less other expenses.

An **INVOICE** is the document a supplier gives a customer when it makes a credit sale to the customer. It shows the customer what amount it owes and when that debt is due to be paid.

A **CREDIT NOTE** is the document a supplier gives a customer when a customer returns items sold on credit. It confirms what goods have been returned, and how much money has been refunded or no longer needs to be paid.

A **PURCHASE ORDER** is the document a customer gives to a supplier requesting that the supplier sells the customer the goods stated on the order.

A **STATEMENT OF ACCOUNT** is the document a supplier sends to a customer to whom it has made credit sales. It shows the total balance the customer owes to the supplier. In other words, it is a list of invoices that have not yet been paid.

A **REMITTANCE ADVICE** is the document a customer sends to a supplier when it pays some of its balance with the supplier, so that the supplier can see exactly which invoices are being paid in that payment.

A **RECEIPT** is the document given to a customer in a cash sale, showing the amount of money the customer paid, and what it related to. You are almost certainly familiar with receipts, as you are given one by a shop every time you go shopping.

A **NUMERICAL CODE** is a code consisting of numbers only.

An **ALPHABETICAL CODE** is a code consisting of letters only.

An **ALPHANUMERICAL CODE** is a code consisting of numbers and letters, in any order.

2

Essential accounting procedures: Test your learning

This chapter gives you question practice on the topics you have covered in the previous chapter. The questions are in the same style you can expect in your assessment. You can find the answers at the back of this Workbook.

1   Organisations have assets, liabilities, income and expenditure.

(a)   **Select the appropriate word from the list of terms below to match the description.**

Description	Term described
An item spent by the organisation.	
An item earned by the organisation.	

List of terms

Income
Liability
Expenditure

(b)   **Select the appropriate word from the list of terms below to match the description.**

Description	Term described
An amount paid to purchase motor insurance.	
A cash sale.	

List of terms

Expenditure
Income
Asset

2   Organisations often make sales and purchases for cash or for credit.

Complete the following sentences by selecting the most appropriate option from the list of terms below.

When an organisation sells goods to a customer and the customer pays for the goods three weeks after the goods are delivered, this is known as a

When an organisation buys services from a person and pays that person on the day the service is carried out, this is known as a

List of terms

Credit sale
Cash sale
Credit purchase
Cash purchase

3   Organisations issue and receive different documents when buying and selling goods.

Complete the following sentences by selecting the most appropriate option from the list of terms below.

An organisation gives [ ] to a customer for goods bought for cash.

An organisation receives [ ] from a supplier listing items returned to the supplier and showing the amount refunded.

An organisation receives [ ] from a customer requesting that the goods specified in the document be sold to the customer.

List of terms

An invoice
A receipt
A purchase order
A credit note

4   You work for Weaver Traders. You are preparing to record some documents in the books of prime entry.

(a)   **Select which ONE of the documents below will be entered in the cash receipts book.**

An invoice received from a supplier ☐

A cheque received from a customer ☐

A credit note received from a supplier ☐

(b)   **Select which ONE of the documents below will be entered in the purchases day book.**

Invoice number 34922 sent to Landy Traders ☐

Invoice number SI9933 sent by AB Supplies ☐

A cheque received from XYZ Traders Ltd ☐

(c)   **Insert an item from the following list into the bottom right hand box of each document below to show which book of prime entry that document will be entered into in Weaver Traders' books. You will not need to use all of the items.**

* Cash payments book
* Cash receipts book
* Purchases day book
* Purchases returns day book
* Sales day book
* Sales returns day book

Weaver Traders
Unit 12, Industrial Park, Beeding, OS17 9DP
VAT registration: 427 4234 00

Invoice number: WT00943   24 March 20XX

To: Tharango Ltd

	£
8 items of product SS2 @ £3.60 each	28.80
VAT @ 20%	5.76
TOTAL	34.56

Book of prime entry [   ]

BPP
LEARNING MEDIA

Gillespie Enterprises

35 High Road, Steeding ST2 9RT
VAT Registration No: 123 4433 00

INVOICE NUMBER: 3546
INVOICE DATE: 6 March 20XX
To: Weaver Traders, Unit 12, Industrial Park, Beeding

	£
4 items of product XX @ £0.99 each	3.96
VAT @ 20%	0.79
Total	4.75

Book of prime entry

National Bank
High Street, Beeding

14-24-19
10534433
Date 14 March 20XX

Pay Gillespie Enterprises only

Four hundred and fifty six pounds and twenty four pence

£456.24

for Weaver Traders

400592   142419   10534433

Book of prime entry

5   Some organisations use coding within the accounting records.

Show whether the following statement is True or False.

In an alphanumerical coding system the code must consist of numbers followed by letters.

True   ☐

False   ☐

6   Your organisation uses a batch processing system to enter purchases invoices into the accounting records.

Show whether the following statement is True or False.

Purchase invoices can be entered into the system together.

True   ☐

False   ☐

7   It is important to ensure that paying-in slips are completed properly.
On 17 April 20XX you are completing a paying-in slip to take to the bank.

(a)   **Which ONE of the following options shows the date as it should be written on the paying-in slip?**

17 April 20XX

17 March 20XX

17.2.XX

(b)   **Which ONE of the following options shows how the three £50 notes you are banking should be shown on the paying-in slip?**

£150

£300

3 × £50

(c)   **Which ONE of the following options shows how the following cheque should be shown on the paying-in slip: Cheque from DS Supplies, £309.35?**

£309.35

£309

£30935

(d) **Show whether the following statement is True or False.**

A paying-in slip should be signed and dated by the person who is paying in the money.

True ☐

False ☐

8 It is 16 April 20XY. You work for Hollands Traders. You have been asked to prepare two cheques for the chief accountant to sign. The cheques will be paying the following balances:

DK Traders £64.87

SG Company £464.82

Complete the TWO cheques below, ready for the chief accountant's signature.

National Bank
National Bank Business Centre, Main Road 14-88-51
44830113

Date _____

Pay _____

_____ only

for Hollands Traders

100346 148851 44830113

National Bank
National Bank Business Centre, Main Road 14-88-51
44830113

Date _____

Pay _____

_____ only

for Hollands Traders

100347 148851 44830113

9   At the end of every year your organisation calculates the profit or loss for the year.

   (a)   **Show whether the following statement is True or False.**

      Income less cost of sales equals gross profit.

      True   ☐

      False   ☐

      Last year your organisation recorded income and expenditure as shown in the table below.

Income and expenditure	£
Sales	377,800
Cost of sales	184,900
Other expenses	94,500

   (b)   **Use the income and expenditure figures to complete the following calculations.**

      (i)   **Calculate gross profit**

         £ ☐

      (ii)   **Calculate net profit**

         £ ☐

3

Mathematics for accounting

Chapter coverage

This chapter covers the unit Mathematics for Accounting and therefore introduces the mathematics you will need to be able to carry out for the purposes of your assessment. This chapter assumes that you will take a calculator to your assessment, which you are expected to do.

1 Using a calculator

Working in an accounting environment, it is important for you to be familiar with a calculator and how it works. Calculators can be simple or complicated, but the basic functions that you will use in this assessment will be the same.

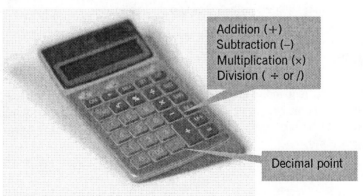

Addition (+)
Subtraction (−)
Multiplication (×)
Division (÷ or /)

Decimal point

2 Addition and subtraction

In your assessment, you will be required to add numbers, both whole numbers and numbers with one or two decimal places.

Money is usually shown to two decimal places, as the numbers before the decimal point indicate the pounds and the numbers after the decimal point indicate the pence.

You may be presented with numbers in columns and have to total them.

How it works

	20,001.20
	10,020.10
	5,200.05
	2,005.02
Total	37,226.37

To add the figures together to come to the total in the shaded box, you should:

1   Enter the first figure carefully into your calculator
2   Press the + button
3   Enter the second figure
4   Press the + button
5   Enter the third figure
6   Press the + button
7   Enter the fourth figure
8   Press the = button

> Ensure you enter figures carefully into your calculator, including the decimal point, or you may make an error.

Try this on the sum above and see if your answer matches ours.

In your assessment, you will be required to subtract or 'take-away' numbers, both whole numbers and numbers with one or two decimal places.

How it works

You may be required to take away (subtract) one number from another, for example, as you learnt in the previous chapters, income take away cost of sales is gross profit. To determine net profit, you would then have to subtract a further number (total other expenditure).

How it works

In the first example below you need to add all the figures to come to the total for parts expenditure at the bottom, which is £182,000. This is adding the column of figures as seen above.

List of parts	£
Part A	25,000
Part B	54,000
Part C	36,000
Part D	67,000
Total (all parts)	

In the next example, below, you need to subtract the three given wages and salaries figures from the total figure given to arrive at the missing administration salaries cost, which is £65,000. The easiest way is to do this in two steps, as shown in the working below the table.

List of wages/salaries costs	£
Factory 1 wages	120,000
Factory 2 wages	140,000
Administration salaries	
Directors' salaries	125,000
Total	450,000

Working

Step one – add the three wages and salaries costs you have been given.

	£
Factory 1 wages	120,000
Factory 2 wages	140,000
Directors' salaries	125,000
Total of costs itemised	385,000

Step two – subtract this figure from the total given in the original table.

	£
Total cost	450,000
Total of costs itemised	(385,000)
Administration salaries	65,000

	£
Income	100,000
Cost of sales	20,000
Other expenditure	15,000

Gross profit = Income – Cost of sales: 100,000 – 20,000 = 80,000

Net profit = Income – Cost of sales – Other expenditure: 100,000 – 20,000 – 15,000 = 65,000

To do this sum on your calculator, you should:

1   Enter the first figure, which is 100,000
2   Press the – button
3   Enter the second figure, which is 20,000
4   Press the – button
5   (The screen may currently show the gross profit figure)
6   Enter the third figure, which is 15,000
7   Press the = button (this will give the net profit figure)

In the assessment, tasks will often ask you to 'calculate', so you must decide if addition or subtraction is required. Often a task will require both functions to be performed, such as when completing missing records (see the How it works example below).

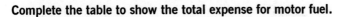

ASK 1 1 Your organisation keeps detailed records of expenses. Motor fuel expenses for each of four delivery vehicles are shown in the table below.

Complete the table to show the total expense for motor fuel.

Delivery vehicles	Motor fuel expense
	£
Vehicle 1	128.42
Vehicle 2	196.55
Vehicle 3	86.09
Vehicle 4	112.42
Total	

2 **Complete the table to show the expense for envelopes.** (Tutorial note: you may need to do this in two steps in a separate working, as shown above.)

Stationery items	Expense
	£
Ink tanks	37.50
Printer paper	18.39
Envelopes	
Pens	7.23
Total	**104.03**

3 Last year your organisation recorded income and expenditure as shown in the table below:

Income and expenditure	
	£
Sales	220,000
Cost of sales	149,000
Wages	26,800
Office expenses	14,600
Selling expenses	19,100

Use the income and expenditure figures to complete the following calculations.

(a)   Calculate gross profit.

£ [   ]

(b)   Calculate net profit.

£ [   ]

4   Last year your organisation recorded income and expenditure as shown in the table below:

Income and expenditure	
	£
Sales	534,000
Cost of sales	302,000
Wages	116,300
Office expenses	52,700
Selling expenses	25,620

Use the income and expenditure figures to complete the following calculations.

(a)   Calculate gross profit.

£ [   ]

(b)   Calculate net profit.

£ [   ]

3 Multiplication and division

In your assessment you could be required to multiply or divide any two numbers, which could be a mixture of whole numbers or numbers with one or two decimal places.

If your answer comes to more than two decimal places, you will need to do what is called 'rounding' to two decimal places. This essentially means leaving off all the numbers after the second decimal place in your answer. All you have to remember is that if the number in the third decimal place in your calculation is 5 or higher, you should increase the number in the second decimal place by 1.

How it works

For example, if your answer is 25.52384, you would present this as 25.52.

If your answer is 25.52684, you would present this as 25.53.

You are likely to be told that an organisation has bought a number of items at a unit price, and to work out the total price. To do this, you must multiply the price by the number of items purchased.

How it works

Your organisation purchased 5 ink cartridges at £24.95 per cartridge from Combes Stationers. **What is the total cost of the ink cartridges?**

To calculate this sum on your calculator, you should:

1   Enter the cost figure, which is 24.95
2   Press the × button
3   Enter the number of cartridges purchased, which is 5
4   Press the = button
5   The screen will now show the total cost of the ink cartridges

Alternatively, you could be told that an organisation has bought a number of items at a total price, and be asked to work out the unit price. To do this, you must divide the total price by the number of items purchased.

How it works

Your organisation purchased 30 reams of paper from Office Suppliers, for a total cost of £74.40. **What is the unit price of one ream of paper?**

To calculate this sum on your calculator, you should:

1   Enter the total cost figure, which is 74.4
2   Press the ÷ button
3   Enter the number of reams purchased, which is 30
4   Press the = button
5   The screen will now show the unit price of a ream of paper

TASK 2 Your organisation purchased 12 bottles of hand soap at £1.25 per bottle from Discount Suppliers.

What is the total cost of the hand soap?

£ [   ]

Your organisation purchased 12 towels from Discount Suppliers, with a total cost of £52.56. **What is the unit price of a towel?**

£ [   ]

4 Ratios

In your assessment, you may have to calculate the ratio of one whole number to another whole number. A ratio will be presented as 'a whole number : a whole number', for example, 3 : 1. This is a way of expressing mathematically that the first number is three times bigger than the second number.

How it works

You are likely to be given a list of costs (for example, stationery items, below), and asked what the ratio of one item to the total or another item is. You may be given a range of ratios and asked which the correct one is, as shown below.

Stationery items	Expense
	£
Ink tanks	25.00
Printer paper	13.29
Envelopes	15.11
Pens	21.60
Total	75.00

Which of the following is the ratio of the total expense for stationery items to the expense for ink tanks?

- 2:1
- 3:1
- 4:1

[   ]

To calculate this, divide the total expense by the expense of ink tanks. On your calculator, you should:

1   Enter the total expense figure, which is 75
2   Press the ÷ button
3   Enter the figure for ink tanks, which is 25
4   Press the = button
5   This gives the answer 3, so the ratio is 3:1. In other words, the total expense is three times bigger than the cost of ink tanks.

ASK 3   Your organisation has the following costs relating to light and heat.

	£
Light	200,000
Heat	100,000
Total	300,000

Which of the following is the ratio of the total cost for light and heat to the cost for heat?

Options

2:1
3:1
4:1

5 Proportions resulting in fractions

In your assessment you might be required to calculate the proportion of one whole number to another whole number and the answer might result in a fraction. This is an expression of the relationship between the two numbers, for example, that directors' salaries equal half of total salary costs for an organisation.

How it works

You could be given the same list of costs as you were given above and asked what proportion of total stationery costs the ink tanks are.

Stationery items	Expense
	£
Ink tanks	25.00
Printer paper	13.29
Envelopes	15.11
Pens	21.60
Total stationery costs	75.00

As the amount for ink tanks is smaller than the total stationery costs, the answer is going to be a fraction. This fraction would be presented initially as $\frac{25}{75}$. However, fractions should always be presented in the smallest numbers possible.

To do this, you need to find a number that both numbers in the fraction can be divided by. In simple cases, the bottom number will be divisible by the top number (which means you will be able to divide the bottom number by the top number and the answer will be a whole number). You should take the following steps:

1   Take the initial fraction $\frac{25}{75}$
2   Determine whether the bottom number can be divided by the top number
3   Enter 75 into the calculator
4   Press the ÷ button
5   Enter 25 into the calculator
6   Press the = button
7   The calculator displays 3

So in this instance, the bottom number *is* divisible by the top number. This can be presented as follows:

$$\frac{25}{75} \div \frac{25}{25} = \frac{1}{3}$$

The answer is therefore $\frac{1}{3}$

There may be occasions when the bottom number cannot be divided by the top number so as to give a whole number. In such cases, you need to find a number that divides into both numbers to give whole numbers for the fraction. Calculations will be fairly simple in your assessment.

How it works

Say the initial fraction was $\frac{4}{10}$. 10 does not divide by 4 to give a whole number, so try and find another number that both 4 and 10 divide by, for example, 2. (The division of 4 and 10 by 2 can be done on a calculator if required.)

$$\frac{4}{10} \div \frac{2}{2} = \frac{2}{5}$$

Remember simple rules, such as even numbers are always divisible by 2. Numbers ending in 5 or 0 are divisible by 5.

You need to continue this process until the numbers cannot be further divided into whole numbers.

How it works

Say the initial fraction was $\frac{18}{30}$. 30 does not divide by 18 to give a whole number, so try and find another number that both 18 and 30 divide by, for example, 3.

$$\frac{18}{30} \div \frac{3}{3} = \frac{6}{10}$$

Remember that you must always divide the top and bottom by the SAME number.

However, 6 and 10 are still both divisible by 2, so the fraction is not being presented in the smallest numbers. Go through the steps again.

$$\frac{6}{10} \div \frac{2}{2} = \frac{3}{5}$$

Now you have reached the point where the numbers will not divide by the same number and remain whole numbers. (Note this could have been done in one step if you had originally chosen to divide 18 and 30 by 6.)

TASK 4 Your organisation has the following costs for catering supplies.

	£
Tea	150
Coffee	250
Milk	350
Total	750

What proportion of the total cost is made up by tea?

6 Percentages

In your assessment, you may be required to calculate what percentage one figure is of another. The answer may be a whole number, or a number to one or two decimal places.

A simple example of a percentage is that 75% of the population drinks tea. What this means is that out of every 100 people in the population, 75 of them drink tea. Accordingly, 25 of them don't, so you could also say that 25% of the population does not drink tea.

Calculating a percentage in this way can give more user-friendly information than if you were told that the population is 61,792,000, of which 46,344,000 drink tea.

In the same way, it might be more useful for directors of an organisation to be told that for every £100 earned, £25 is gross profit (25%) rather than just being told that for total income of £37,794,584, gross profit is £9,448,646.

How it works

You might be given figures for sales, cost of sales and gross profit (or previously have been asked to calculate gross profit), for example:

	£
Sales	120,000
Cost of sales	90,000
Gross profit	30,000

You may then be asked to calculate gross profit as a percentage of sales. To calculate this on your calculator, you should:

1   Enter the gross profit figure, which is 30,000
2   Press the ÷ button
3   Enter the sales figure, which is 120,000
4   Press the = button
5   The screen should show a figure after the decimal place 0.25
6   Press the × button
7   Enter 100
8   Press the = button
9   The screen will show the percentage figure (in this case, 25%). In other words, for every £100 earned, the organisation makes £25 gross profit.

Alternatively, you may be given a figure (for example, a sales price) and be told that it is going to increase by a certain percentage. You may be asked what the amount of the increase is.

How it works

You might be told that the sales price for Part AB23 is £4.80 and that it is going to increase by 5%. You could be required to calculate the amount of the rise.

The best way to understand this is to say that £4.80 is 100%. You can calculate what 1% is by dividing the price by 100. You can then find 5% by multiplying by 5. To calculate the figure, you therefore need to:

1   Enter the existing price, which is 4.80
2   Press the ÷ button
3   Enter 100
4   Press the = button
5   The screen shows 1%, which is 0.048
6   Press the × button
7   Enter 5
8   Press the = button
9   The screen shows 5%, which is 0.24

The increase is 24 pence (you would show this in the assessment as £0.24).

TASK 5 (a)   Your organisation has produced the following figures for the year.

	£
Sales	253,700
Cost of sales	190,275
Gross profit	63,425

Calculate gross profit as a percentage of sales.

[   ] %

(b)   The current selling price of part DC45IT is £569. This is going to increase by 3%.

Calculate the increase in the selling price.

£ [   ]

7 Fractions

Similarly in your assessment, you might be asked to apply a fraction to a whole number. This may give an answer which is a whole number, or a number to one or two decimal places.

How it works

You might be told the current selling price of an item and be told that it is going to rise by a fraction. For example, the current selling price of part AX345 is £36. It is going to rise by $\frac{1}{6}$. What is the increase in selling price for part AX345?

To calculate this figure on your calculator, you need to:

1   Enter the existing price, which is 36
2   Press the × button
3   Enter the top number in the fraction, which is 1
4   Press the ÷ button
5   Enter the bottom number in the fraction, which is 6
6   Press the = button
7   The screen shows the increase in the selling price, which is 6

> Steps 2 and 3 are NOT absolutely necessary when the top number of the fraction is 1, but are necessary if the top number is higher than 1, for example where the fraction is 2/3.

TASK 6 (a)   The current selling price of part XZ20 is £49. This is going to increase by $\frac{1}{7}$.

Calculate the increase in the selling price.

£ [   ]

(b)   The current selling price of part CVB34 is £25. This is going to increase by $\frac{2}{5}$.

Calculate the increase in the selling price.

£ [   ]

8 Averages

In your assessment, you may have to calculate the average value of a range of numbers up to five numbers. The answer may be a whole number or a number with one or two decimal places. The average cost of five units for instance is the total cost divided by the number of elements making up that cost (5), that is what the individual unit cost would be if they were all the same. It is critical therefore to work out how many elements make up the total in order to do the calculation.

How it works

You may be given a range of costs, with a total, and asked what the average cost is. For example, the following are the costs of wages per department in your organisation. There are four elements (departments) making up the total cost.

	£
Department 1	253,049
Department 2	645,900
Department 3	234,984
Department 4	302,845
Total	1,436,778

To calculate the average cost per department on your calculator, you need to:

1   Enter the total cost, which is 1,436,778
2   Press the ÷ button
3   Enter the total number of departments being averaged (in this case 4)
4   Press the = button
5   The screen should show the average cost per department, which is 359,194.50

The key thing to remember when calculating an average is that the number you divide by is the number of things being averaged. This will never be more than 5 in your assessment, but could be 2, 3 or 4 as well.

TASK 7   The following table shows the number of miles driven by the three delivery vehicles belonging to your organisation during the year.

Delivery vehicles	Mileage
	£
Vehicle 1	2,645
Vehicle 2	1,035
Vehicle 3	895
Total	4,575

Calculate the average number of miles driven by the delivery vehicles.

	miles

Chapter overview

Working in an accounting environment, it is important for you to be familiar with a calculator and how it works.

In your assessment, you will be required to add numbers, both whole numbers and numbers with up to two decimal places.

Money is usually shown to two decimal places, as the numbers before the decimal point indicate the pounds and the numbers after the decimal point indicate the pence.

Ensure you enter figures carefully into your calculator, including the decimal point, or you may make an error.

In your assessment, you will be required to subtract numbers, both whole numbers and those with up to two decimal places.

Tasks will often ask you to 'calculate', so you must determine if addition or subtraction is required.

In your assessment, you could be required to multiply or divide any two numbers, which could be a mixture of whole numbers or numbers with one or two decimal places.

If your answer comes to more than two decimal places, you will need to do what is called 'rounding' to two decimal places.

In your assessment, you may have to calculate the ratio of one whole number to another whole number. A ratio will be presented as 'a whole number : a whole number' (for example, 3:1). This is a way of expressing mathematically that the first number is three times bigger than the second number.

In your assessment, you might be required to calculate the proportion of one whole number to another whole number and the answer might result in a fraction.

This is an expression of the relationship between the two numbers, for example, that directors' salaries equal half of total salary costs at an organisation.

Fractions should always be presented in the smallest numbers possible.

In your assessment, you will be required to calculate what percentage one figure is of another. The answer may be a whole number, or a number with one or two decimal places.

Alternatively, you may be given a figure (for example, a sales price) and be told that it is going to increase by a certain percentage.

In your assessment, you might be asked to apply a fraction to a whole number. This may give an answer which is a whole number, or a number with one or two decimal places.

In your assessment, you may have to calculate the average value of a range of numbers up to five numbers. The answer may be a whole number or a number with one or two decimal places.

This chapter gives you question practice on the topics you have covered in the previous chapter. The questions are in the same style you can expect in your assessment. You can find the answers at the back of this Workbook.

1   Your organisation sold 2 cars for £958.30 in total to Super Car Traders.

    (a)   **What is the average price of each car?**

       £ [   ]

    Super Car Traders paid for the cars when they collected them.

    (b)   **Is the sale of the cars a cash transaction or a credit transaction?**

       [   ]

2   Last year your organisation recorded income and expenditure as shown in the table below.

Income and expenditure	£
Sales	577,500
Cost of sales	285,900
Other expenses	197,583

    (a)   **Use the income and expenditure figures to complete the following calculations.**

       (i)   **Calculate gross profit**

          £ [   ]

(ii)   **Calculate net profit**

£ _____

(b)   **Using your answer from (a)(ii), calculate net profit as a percentage of sales. If your answer is not a whole number make sure you give your answer to two decimal places.**

_____ %

3   An organisation is reviewing the selling price of some of its products.

The current selling price of product number 52 is £17.00. This is to be increased by $\frac{1}{5}$ (one fifth).

(a)   **Calculate the increase in selling price for product number 52.**

£ _____

The current selling price of product number 12 is £18.00. This is to be increased by 6%.

(b)   **Calculate the increase in selling price for product number 12.**

£ _____

4   An organisation is reviewing the selling price of some of its products.

The current selling price of product number 104 is £62. This is to be increased by $\frac{1}{8}$.

(a)   **Calculate the increase in selling price for product number 104.**

£ _____

The current selling price of product number AZ25 is £9. This is to be increased by 6%.

(b)   **Calculate the increase in selling price for product number AZ25.**

£ _____

5   Your organisation keeps detailed records of sales.

Sales at each of four outlets are shown in the table below.

(a)   **Complete the table to show the sales at Outlet 4.**

Sales per outlet	£
Outlet 1	250,368.25
Outlet 2	199,473.79
Outlet 3	302,699.39
Outlet 4	
Total	1,127,751.60

(b)   **Calculate the average sales per outlet.**

£

Analysed sales at Outlet 1 are shown in the table below.

(c)   **Complete the table to show the sales from menswear.**

Item	£
Menswear	
Ladieswear	61,506
Childrenswear	62,595
Household fabrics	50,076
Total	250,380

(d)   **Which of the following is the ratio of total sales at Outlet 1 to sales of childrenswear at Outlet 1?**

- 4:1
- 5:1
- 6:1

(e)   **Which of the following is the proportion of the total sales at Outlet 1 made up by household fabrics?**

- ▪ $\dfrac{1}{5}$

- ▪ $\dfrac{1}{6}$

- ▪ $\dfrac{1}{7}$

[ ]

6   Your organisation keeps detailed records of costs.

Costs at each of two premises are shown in the table below.

(a)   **Complete the table to show the costs at Premises 2.**

Costs per premises	£
Premises 1	50,924.72
Premises 2	
Total	102,049.94

(b)   **Calculate the average cost of each premises.**

£ [ ]

Analysed costs at Premises 1 are shown in the table below.

Item	£
Cost of sales	34,368
Distribution costs	6,372
Administration costs	10,185
Total	50,925

(c)   **Which of the following is the ratio of total costs to administration costs?**

- ▪   4:1
- ▪   5:1
- ▪   6:1

5

Accounting in a professional environment

1 Types of organisation

So far in this Workbook you have considered a very simple business model – an organisation that buys and sells items trying to make profit.

There are many organisations that exist to make a profit, but there are also organisations with different aims. Organisations fall into what are called different sectors.

> **KEYWORDS**
>
> Organisations in the **private sector** aim to make a profit.
>
> Organisations in the **public sector** and the **charitable sector** have different aims, and making a profit may not be the most important of them.

How it works

The table below shows the types of organisations that fall into each of these sectors.

Private sector	Limited companies
	Partnerships
	Sole traders
Public sector	Councils (local government)
	National Health Service (NHS)
	Fire and Ambulance Service
	Police Service
Charitable sector	Charities – for example, Oxfam, Save the Children

At this stage of your studies, you do not need to know anything more about these types of organisation, only the sectors they are in, and the main purpose of organisations in those sectors.

TASK 1 Fill in the gaps in the sentences below, using words given in the options below. You may have to use the same word more than once.

Limited companies aim to make a

The National Health Service does not exist to make a

Options

Profit

Cost saving

2 The accounting function

KEYWORD

The accounting function is one of the departments in an organisation.

The accounting function may be a large department with many staff, or it may be one individual – the organisation's accountant. It exists to support the organisation, by recording transactions and providing information to its customers.

KEYWORD

The customers of the accounting function are other departments of the organisation (for example, production, sales), external trade customers of the organisation and suppliers of the organisation.

How it works

Customers of the accounting function of ABC Traders

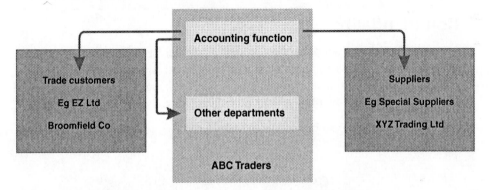

The accounting function of ABC Traders serves these parties (customers).

- It sends invoices and statements of account to trade customers
- It sends payments and remittance advice to suppliers
- It sends information to other departments of ABC Traders

The accounting function also holds the following information which it may supply to other departments:

- Information about whether the organisation is making a profit or loss
- Information about actual income (also compared with expected income)
- Information about actual expenditure (also compared with expected expenditure)

Managers in the organisation use the information given to them by the accounting function to make better business decisions and to enable them to run their departments.

When an accounting function provides information to another department in the organisation, it is important that it is **complete, timely and accurate**, to enable managers to use it to run the organisation **effectively** and **efficiently**.

TASK 2 1   **Give three examples of customers of the accounting function.**

2   **Fill in the gaps in the following statement.**

The accounting function provides [   ] to other

departments in the organisation. This should be [   ],

[   ] and timely to ensure that managers in the

organisation can make better business decisions.

---

3 Confidentiality

The type of information produced by an accounting function for other departments is very often sensitive, that is the organisation could be harmed if it was made public. The organisation needs to keep that information private, in other words secret, within the organisation. Another word for this privacy is **confidentiality.**

> **KEYWORD**
>
> Confidentiality is the concept of keeping sensitive information private.

Why might a business want to keep information confidential?

Customers might not be happy at the amount of profit that the organisation makes on sales to them, and buy them from someone else...

Suppliers might not be happy at the amount of profit that the organisation makes on items they sell to the organisation, so they may raise their prices, or attempt to cut out the organisation and sell direct to its customers...

If sensitive information becomes public knowledge, it can be very damaging to the organisation and even affect whether it can continue trading.

There is even information produced by an organisation that it might not want its own staff to know:

The accounting function might have access to such information, but have to keep it confidential until top management want it to be public in the organisation.

So how does an organisation keep information confidential?

How it works

Small practical issues are extremely important. For example:

Keeping sensitive files locked up

Not leaving work on your desk when you leave your desk, even for a few moments

Password protecting computer files

Locking your computer screen when you leave your desk, even for a few moments

Careful disposal of documentation once it is no longer required to be kept   .

Giving staff working on sensitive issues private offices

Many accounts departments are open plan, but people with certain key roles are likely to have private space to work in:

- The finance controller (likely to have access to confidential, director-level information)

- The wages clerk (access to confidential personnel information)

There are laws governing disclosure of personal information (for example, the type of information an employee might have on a personnel file) and therefore this sort of information must be kept confidential too. People working in an accounting function might have access to such personal information and so must take care to keep it confidential, by keeping files private and safe as outlined above.

TASK 3 **List three ways that someone dealing with confidential information can keep that information secret.**

1 ....

2 ....

3 ....

4 Ethics and professional behaviour

KEYWORD

Ethics is another word for rules of behaviour.

Accountants and people who work in an accounting function are expected to conform to particular rules of behaviour, because organisations and individuals rely on the information they produce to make important decisions.

The key aspects of these rules for people working in an accounting function are that those people should be:

- **Honest** (sometimes called having integrity or being straightforward)

- **Up to date** in the technical knowledge they need to do their job (for example, knowing about the most recent accounting standards)

Keeping sensitive information confidential is another important rule of behaviour for those working in an accounting function.

ASK 4   **Accountants must keep training throughout their careers, to keep up to date with changes in accounting during their career.**

True   ☐

False   ☐

5 Social and environmental behaviour

It is not just people who need to behave in a responsible manner. Organisations themselves have an important role in society, and their production processes and business operations may have a large impact on the environment.

The managers of organisations want people to have a good impression of them. This is unlikely to be the case if an organisation has just caused an environmental disaster.

Most organisations do not deal in products that are likely to cause a major environmental disaster, but all organisations can take small steps to reduce what impact they do have on the environment.

How it works

Positive environmental policies

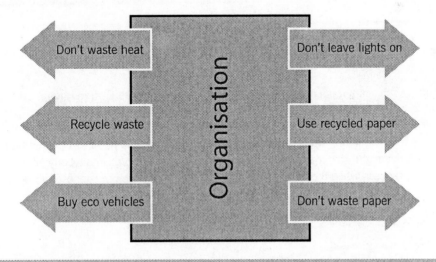

TASK 5 **Place a tick (✓) in the boxes to indicate which THREE of the following are sensible social and environmental policies for an organisation to adopt.**

- Don't use paper ☐
- Don't waste electricity ☐
- Don't use unleaded fuel ☐
- Don't buy fuel inefficient vehicles ☐
- Don't pay employees ☐
- Don't leave lights on in unoccupied premises ☐

6 Health and safety

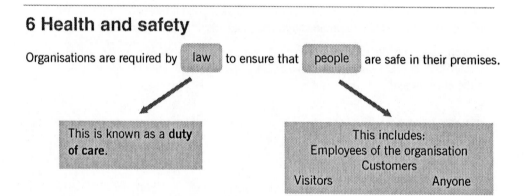

Organisations are required by | law | to ensure that | people | are safe in their premises.

This is known as a **duty of care**.

This includes:
Employees of the organisation
Customers
Visitors   Anyone

KEYWORD

A **duty of care** is a legal responsibility. Organisations are required to have made an effort to ensure anyone on their premises is not at risk.

For example, if building work was taking place and a large hole had been dug in the floor to be left overnight, the organisation has a duty to fence it to protect anybody who goes into the premises while the hole is there, even if the people are not supposed to be there.

The duty extends to employees of the organisation, who are required to

behave in a safe manner

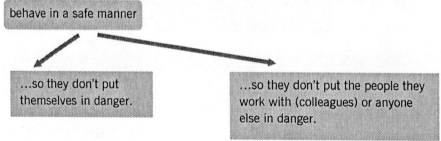

...so they don't put themselves in danger.

...so they don't put the people they work with (colleagues) or anyone else in danger.

How it works

Examples of what would be unsafe behaviour:

> Trailing wires from a workstation across corridors or walkways

> Smoking near flammable items

> Being careless with liquids near computer or other electrical equipment

> Overloading an electric socket with electric points

> Leaving piles of paper and files on the floor for colleagues to trip over

> This could also lead to inefficient working practices. See below.

An employee in the accounting function has a duty to support the organisation by reporting any unsafe practices to a supervisor. Such employees should also set an example in their tidy work areas. This also contributes to efficient working practices, see below.

TASK 6 **Select the appropriate words in each of the following sentences.**

John has seen Rashid smoking in the stationery cupboard. He [should] [should not] report this to his supervisor.

Karen is visiting Total Traders. Total Traders [does] [does not] have a duty to ensure Karen is safe during her visit.

Amandeep has asked maintenance to increase the number of electric points at her desk. They have not yet done so. Amandeep [should] [should not] use an adaptor brought in from home to enable her to use all her electronic equipment at the same time.

7 Efficient working practices

As noted above, keeping a tidy workstation contributes to efficient working practices. This is because time is wasted if files or documents take a long time to find because they are not filed properly, or there is not space on the desk for the person in the accounting function to actually do any work!

KEYWORD

Efficiency is functioning in the best possible manner with the least waste of time and effort.

How it works

Efficient working is affected by different things:

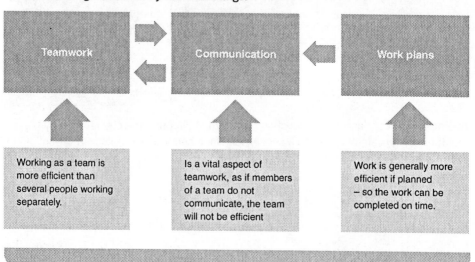

Teamwork	Communication	Work plans
Working as a team is more efficient than several people working separately.	Is a vital aspect of teamwork, as if members of a team do not communicate, the team will not be efficient	Work is generally more efficient if planned – so the work can be completed on time.

KEYWORD

A work plan, in simple terms, is a list or a record of work that an individual or group intends to do, often ordered in terms of priority that each element of that work is given.

How it works

Work plans take many forms, for example:

- To do lists
- Diaries
- In trays – a place to collect incoming documents that require your attention
- Schedules

Work plans are important in their own right because they help individuals work efficiently. However, they also tie into communication within the team, because if work is planned and that plan is written down, team members can access the plan if needed, for example, if a team member is ill, and re-assign work, to continue to work efficiently as a team.

It is rare in an accounting function for someone to work in isolation. Usually one person depends on work being done by another person if they are to carry out their own work.

How it works

For example, if the sales clerk does not process the invoices, the credit controller does not have an up to date record of who owes money when. As another example, if the purchases clerk does not process the invoices, the payments clerk does not know who to pay when.

This is why communication is vital, because if one person is going to miss a deadline, it might mean that everyone in the team goes on to miss their deadlines, and the work of the whole function becomes inefficient.

If individuals who are having problems meeting deadlines communicate with the rest of their team, contingency plans (back-up plans) can be made and other members of the team can contribute to enable that deadline to be met. The same is true if a team of people in the accounting function is not going to meet a deadline required by another department.

It may be important that an individual in a team assists another team member with work that the first individual would not usually do in order to keep the whole team efficient. This would not be the case if confidentiality were affected but a team member might be able to assist a struggling team member by answering the phone, taking over administration tasks, or proof-reading a non-confidential letter or report.

How it works

A junior clerk is not likely to help the payroll clerk to produce the payroll as they might not have the skills to do so, and confidentiality could be affected. However, if the payroll clerk is experiencing difficulty meeting deadlines, the junior clerk could take over any non-confidential tasks, such as answering the phone or printing out documents.

TASK 7 **Which THREE of the following statements are true?**

- A member of the accounting function should keep a tidy desk to ensure efficient working practices.

- A member of the accounting function should communicate with the team about meeting deadlines.

- A member of the accounting function should keep his or her work diary confidential.

- A member of the accounting function should communicate with the team to contribute to their work efficiency.

TASK 8 It is important to work effectively.

Answer the following questions by selecting the most appropriate option.

It is Tuesday lunchtime and you have a normal workload remaining for the week. Your colleague needs to go to an important meeting in 30 minutes, but is also working on a key report which needs to be processed before the end of the day.

Which ONE of the following actions should you take?

☐ Continue with your work to ensure that you meet your deadlines and leave early if you have the opportunity.

☐ Go to your colleague and ask her if there is anything you could do to help her meet her deadline.

☐ Recommend the colleague just submits the report without further checking so she meets the deadline.

8 Personal skills and development

We have already touched on certain skills that someone working in the accounting function needs, namely honesty, integrity, technical knowledge and organisation. There are various other skills required too:

- Reliability
- Being numerate (able with numbers)
- Punctuality
- Willingness to learn (and continue learning)
- Good communication skills (as discussed above)

A person working in an accounting function is likely to have these skills in order to have got the job, but it is also important to continually improve these skills and, as discussed before, continue learning.

Personal development can be achieved through formal training – for example gaining qualifications and attending training courses. It can also be achieved through more informal ways, for example by reading relevant literature (accountancy magazines) or by watching how more senior members of staff do their job.

How it works

Development method	
AAT qualification	This is formal training involving passing assessments in order to obtain the qualification.
Training courses	This is formal training involving being taught the information required to pass the assessments referred to above. This may be in a classroom, or by use of a home learning package.
On the job training	This is formal training (it tends to be more practical than the two other examples of formal training given above).
Job rotation	This can be formal training. Many apprentices or trainees are required to work in more than one area in an accounts department or business during their training period to help them gain an overview of the processes of the organisation (by 'rotating' between areas).

Development method	
Job shadowing	This can be formal or informal. It involves watching another member of staff do their job to learn how it is done. This may be done as a formal part of training or simply informally as a junior clerk learns from those around him or her.
Self-study: for example, reading journals or books or researching something on the Internet.	This is informal learning that a person can do to improve their own knowledge and abilities and to complement formal training undertaken as outlined above.

9 Managers and mentors

Both methods of acquiring learning outlined above can be improved by the involvement of a supervisor and/or mentor.

> **KEYWORDS**
>
> A **supervisor** is a manager who oversees a process (in this case, the training of a junior staff member).
>
> A **mentor** is a trusted advisor and guide who adds value to the training process, either by undertaking teaching personally or by directing the trainee to the best training options for that trainee.

Training should be discussed with a supervisor before being carried out, and also afterwards, in the form of an appraisal, so that the supervisor can ensure the training was understood. In addition, a supervisor will ensure that the training is relevant to, and used in, the organisation. Ideally a supervisor will arrange that a person's practical work and their formal training are in harmony so that what is being learnt is being used in practice. Then by monitoring the person's work, a supervisor can further identify whether the training is being understood.

A mentor can:

- Discuss training needs and make recommendations
- Carry out or arrange relevant training (in conjunction with the supervisor)

It is possible that one person could undertake both supervisor and mentoring roles for someone. It could also be the case that an individual has a supervisor at work, and a mentor connected with the formal classroom learning side of training.

TASK 9 **Select the appropriate word in each of the following sentences.**

A person training in an accounting function should | should not discuss training

needs with their supervisor.

A person who wants a job in an accounting function should be punctual | pleasant .

Chapter overview

There are many organisations that exist to make a profit, but there are also organisations with different aims.

Organisations fall into different sectors (private, public and charitable).

The accounting function is one of the departments in an organisation.

The customers of the accounting function are other departments of the organisation (for example, production, sales), external trade customers of the organisation and suppliers of the organisation.

The accounting function provides information to its customers.

Information should be complete, accurate and timely to be useful to users.

Managers use the information given to them by the accounting function to make better business decisions and work effectively and efficiently.

Some information must be kept private, that is, confidential.

Practical steps such as password protecting documents and keeping files locked up will help keep information confidential.

Some personal information must be kept private and people working in the accounting function must ensure this is done, by using the same practical methods of for instance locking files and using passwords.

Members of the accounting function must abide by certain rules of conduct.

In particular, they should be honest and keep up to date with technical knowledge.

Organisations should take steps to reduce their impact on the environment.

Organisations are required by law to ensure that people are safe in their premises.

The duty extends to employees of the organisation, who are required to behave in a safe manner.

An employee in the accounting function has a duty to support the organisation by reporting any unsafe practices to a supervisor.

Efficiency is affected by teamwork, communication and work plans.

Someone working in the accounting function needs integrity, technical knowledge and organisation, reliability, punctuality, willingness to learn (and continue learning), good communication skills and to be numerate.

Continuing training can be formal or informal.

Training should be arranged and reviewed in consultation with a supervisor.

The supervisor can ensure that training is used to the benefit of the individual and the organisation and that training is understood, by supervising the ongoing work of that individual.

A mentor can add value to training by tailoring it to the individual's needs.

Keywords

Organisations in the **PRIVATE SECTOR** aim to make a profit.

Organisations in the **PUBLIC SECTOR** and the **CHARITABLE SECTOR** have different aims, and making a profit may not be the most important of them.

The **ACCOUNTING FUNCTION** is one of the departments in an organisation.

The **CUSTOMERS OF THE ACCOUNTING FUNCTION** are other departments of the organisation (for example, production, sales), external trade customers of the organisation and suppliers of the organisation.

CONFIDENTIALITY is the concept of keeping sensitive information private.

ETHICS is another word for rules of conduct.

A **DUTY OF CARE** is a legal responsibility. Organisations are required to have made an effort to ensure anyone on their premises is not at risk.

EFFICIENCY is functioning in the best possible manner with the least waste of time and effort.

A **WORK PLAN**, in simple terms, is a list or a record of work that an individual or group intends to do, possibly ordered in terms of the priority that each element of that work is given.

A **SUPERVISOR** is a manager who oversees a process such as the training of a junior staff member.

A **MENTOR** is a trusted advisor and guide who adds value to the training process, either by undertaking teaching personally or by directing the trainee to the best training options for that trainee.

This chapter gives you question practice on the topics you have covered in the previous chapter. The questions are in the same style you can expect in your assessment. You can find the answers at the back of this Workbook.

1   There are different types of organisation.

Complete the following sentences by selecting the most appropriate option from the list of items below each sentence.

(a)   A sole trader is a [   ] organisation.

   ▪   private sector
   ▪   public sector
   ▪   charitable

(b)   The police service [   ] aim to make a profit.

   ▪   does
   ▪   does not

2   It is important to understand the role of the accounting department within an organisation.

   Show whether the following statements are True or False.

   ✳ (a)   Detailed expenditure analysis provided by the accounting department is used by the general public to make business decisions.

   True   ☐

   False   ☐

(b)   An example of a customer of the accounting department is the organisation's suppliers.

True   ☐

False   ☐

3   It is important to observe confidentiality.

Complete the following sentences by inserting the most appropriate option from the list below each sentence.

Information about pay increases held on a computer should be kept

☐

- in an area to which all employees have access.
- in a password protected file with access restricted to those who need the information.

A supplier of the organisation where you work asks you who the main customers of the organisation are. You reply:

☐

- 'I am sorry but I cannot give you any information as it is confidential.'
- 'As you are a supplier I can tell you that it is Matlins and Swindells.'

4   Finance professionals and organisations have a duty to behave in a professional and socially responsible manner.

Show whether the following statements are True or False.

Accountants should behave with integrity in all circumstances.

True   ☐

False   ☐

✳ Organisations can behave in a socially irresponsible manner because they have no responsibility to the general public.

True   ☐

False   ☐

5   Organisations should observe health and safety guidelines.

(a)   **Complete this sentence by inserting the most appropriate option from the list below each box.**

An organisation [   ] provide a safe environment for [   ]

<table>
<tr><td>must</td><td>staff and customers only</td></tr>
<tr><td>does not have to</td><td>anyone on the premises</td></tr>
</table>

(b)   **Show whether the following statements are True or False.**

An employee has a duty not to put him or herself in danger at work.

True   ☐

False   ☐

It is important to keep a tidy desk to ensure you work efficiently.

True   ☐

False   ☐

6   It is important to understand the skills and attributes needed by a finance professional.

(a)   **Complete this sentence by inserting the most appropriate option from the list below each box.**

A finance professional should [   ] and be [   ]

<table>
<tr><td>communicate well</td><td>reactionary</td></tr>
<tr><td>communicate rarely</td><td>reliable</td></tr>
</table>

✳ (b)   **Show whether the following statements are True or False.**

Training for the AAT qualification is the only appropriate method of formal training for a finance professional.

True   ☐

False   ☐

One reason somebody training to be a finance professional discusses training needs with their supervisor is so that the supervisor can make recommendations.

True   ☐

False   ☐

7   It is important to work effectively.

(a) **Answer the following questions by selecting the most appropriate option.**

It is Wednesday lunchtime and you have a report that needs to be processed by the end of the day. You are well behind with the report and it is unlikely that you will complete it in time. You have a colleague that has an ordinary workload for the rest of the week.

Which ONE of the following actions should you take?

☐   Tell no-one as you don't want to appear inefficient

☐   Ask your colleague if she is able to spare any time to help you meet the deadline

☐   Tell your supervisor that you will definitely meet the deadline.

Planning is very important to help you meet your deadlines.

(b) **Which ONE of the following documents below is a planning aid?**

☐   Schedule

☐   Purchase order

☐   Paying in slip

7

Creating business documents

Chapter coverage

This chapter introduces the unit Creating Business Documents. It introduces the key issues you need to know for your assessment.

1 Business documents

You were introduced to some business documents in Chapter 1:

- Invoices
- Credit notes
- Statements of account
- Remittance advice

These documents are the main way that organisations communicate with their customers and suppliers.

Routine business documents (such as invoices, remittances) will be sent to customers and suppliers. Other business documents may be sent to other parties associated with the business, known as stakeholders.

Stakeholders are people or groups that have an interest in the organisation.

How it works

Examples of such interested parties are:

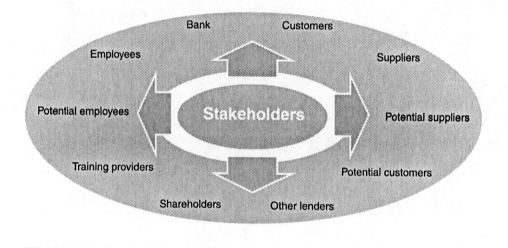

Other common forms of business communication

An email is an electronic form of communication which may be sent both within and outside of the organisation.

A letter is a written form of communication usually sent outside of the organisation.

A memo is a relatively informal written form of communication sent from one employee to another within the same organisation.

A report is a relatively formal written form of communication which can be sent from one employee to another within the same organisation or outside of the organisation.

How it works

Letters	Emails	Reports	Memos

Some examples of these types of communication from a company called Haywood Distributors are given below. DO NOT WORRY about the content of these communications, they are to illustrate what each looks like only. Key elements of each communication have been pointed out. These will be looked at in further detail below in the section about creating business documents.

Letter

Headed paper including the company name and address

HAYWOOD DISTRIBUTORS

Industrial Estate
Haywood
HY4 2SK

Indication letter is for addressee only

CONFIDENTIAL

J M Jones
Administrator
Pursel Retail Ltd
Pear Tree Lane Industrial Estate
Sussex BN1 4PW

Addressee and his address

Date

3 September 20X0

Dear Mr Jones,

Uses polite form of his name as letter is formal

Introductory sentence outlinin what letter is about

Account No 0139742

Thank you for your letter of 28 August 20X0 regarding credit payments owing to your account as a result of product returns.

I have looked into the matter that you raised and I am afraid that your earlier letter of 26 July was indeed overlooked, due to the temporary absence of the member of staff to whom you addressed it.

Body o dealin the is

I apologise for the delay in processing your credit payment. I have arranged for your account to be credited with the sum of £346.99, and I enclose a print-out of your account status confirming the balance.

If you have any further queries, please do not hesitate to contact me.

Yours sincerely,

Your Name

Signature

Courteous closing sentence

Assistant Financial Accountant

Appropriate sign off for use with person's name at outset of letter

Title of person sending the letter (the signatory)

Email

EMAIL

Recipient

ksaltmarsh@haywooddistributors.co.uk

Sender

cfrancis@haywooddistributors.co.uk

8 July 20X8

Date

Sales variances – June

Subject matter

In response to your query, the following sales variances by product type were incurred in June:

Simple introduction

Product	Variance
MP3 players	£14,300 adverse
Portable DVD players	£2,700 favourable
DVD/VHS combo players	£21,600 adverse
Digital TVs	£18,600 favourable

Information required

If you require further detail, please let me know.

Courteous sign off

Clare

'Signature'

Report

Headed paper

Title of report

HAYWOOD DISTRIBUTORS

REPORT: COMPLIANCE WITH POLICY & PROCEDURE

TO: Department Heads — *Recipients*

FROM: Jenny Faulkner, Financial Accountant — *Report writer (including their position)*

DATE: 3 September 20X0 — *Date*

1   Introduction — *Introduction*

This report was compiled by Your Name, Accounts Clerk, at the request of Jenny Faulkner, Financial Accountant, and submitted on 3rd September 20X0.

2   Non-compliance with policy and procedure   *Main issue in report*

In recent months, I have witnessed several cases in which staff members failed to comply with formal policies and procedures.

- Cheque requisition forms have had to be returned to the originators because they were incorrectly completed or authorised. (See copies attached: Appendix 1.)

- There is an apparent lack of respect for the confidentiality of other staff members' personal details, in verbal and written communication with third parties.

- Staff members fail to take part in fire evacuation drills, and when they do take part, fail to comply with proper procedures (eg by taking lifts and leaving fire doors open). (See the Safety Officer's report on the most recent drill: Appendix 2.)

3   Reasons for concern   *Implications of main issue in report*

I believe these 'lapses' in compliance are of concern, for several reasons.

Policies and procedures, such as the ones mentioned, have been put in place to ensure the efficiency of operations such as cheque requisition; the confidentiality of information which may be used to the detriment of the organisation and/or its staff; and the safety of staff and visitors in the event of an emergency.

Non-compliance in such areas jeopardises efficiency (by necessitating re-work), data security and personal safety.

By themselves these may be small things, but I believe they may reflect a culture of 'corner cutting' which may eventually result in more serious consequences.

Recommendations for improvements

4	**How Haywood can improve compliance**

I would like to make the following recommendations for management's consideration.

- All staff should be reminded of their responsibility to comply with organisational policies and procedures.

- Where necessary, training should be given to reinforce awareness and competence in relevant procedures.

- Managers at all levels should seek to monitor and enforce compliance more strictly, and to model compliance in their own conduct.

I hope this information is helpful, and I would be willing to discuss it further – and to present more detailed evidence of my observations – at your convenience.

Courteous sign off

Appendix 1: Incorrectly completed cheque requisition forms (attached)
Appendix 2: Safety Officer's Report for August 20X0 (attached)

List of appendices (appendices themselves not given here)

Memo

Recipient

MEMO

To:	[Recipient's name, designation]	**Reference:**	[File reference]
From:	[Sender's name, designation]	**Date:**	[In full]
Subject:	[Concise statement of main theme or topic of message]		

Date

Subject matter

Sender

The main text of the memo is set out in correct, concise, readily understandable English, in spaced paragraphs following a clear, logical structure. Note that no inside address, salutation or complimentary close are required.

Signature or initials [optional]

Using the right form of communication

So when is it appropriate to use each form of communication?

The answer depends on the relationship between the two parties communicating and the nature of the business being carried out.

In general terms, the formality of these forms of communication goes from informal to formal as follows:

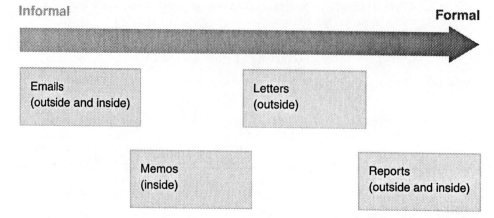

Informal   **Formal**

Emails
(outside and inside)

Letters
(outside)

Memos
(inside)

Reports
(outside and inside)

Note also whether the documents are used inside the organisation or outside. It is these details which will help you decide when each form of communication is appropriate.

How it works

Tracey has been asked to send a product sample to a customer. You need to determine the most appropriate form of communication to send with this sample. You can take a number of steps to work this out.

1   Eliminate obviously wrong options

In this case, an email would be inappropriate, as the sample needs to be physically sent by traditional mail.

2   Determine if the communication is internal or external

In this case, the communication is external, so a memo would be inappropriate.

3   Consider the purpose of the communication

In this case, the purpose of the communication is to be polite. The customer does not need any additional information other than the price list. Therefore, a formal report would be inappropriate.

In this case, by process of elimination, we have determined that the appropriate method of communication is a letter.

ASK 1   1   A written form of communication usually sent outside of the organisation is

A memo   ☐

An email   ☐

A letter   ☐

2   John has been asked to check that everyone in the sales department is able to attend an important meeting on 25 February 20XX. It is 23 February now. The most appropriate method of communication for him to use is

A memo   ☐

An email   ☐

A letter   ☐

A report   ☐

2 Templates and house style

> **KEYWORD**
>
> A template is a standard for business documents, such as invoices and credit notes, so that all such documents issued by a business look the same, and are instantly recognisable for what they are.

Organisations use templates to benefit themselves and their customers and suppliers. If the receiving party knows exactly what a document is and who it is from, they can process it quickly and easily. This should mean that the organisation receives what it wants promptly too (for example, payment, in the case of a sales invoice, or goods, in the case of an order).

> **KEYWORD**
>
> 'House style' is an expression of how the organisation wants to present itself in its communications.

It may include:

- The use of standardised letterheads and memo pads
- How letters and memos are laid out
- What headings and formats are used for reports
- The logos, typefaces and colours used as part of the corporate identity

How it works

For example, at Haywood Distributors, there is a house style manual for all communications sent to external parties.

Standardised stationery is available for handwritten and word-processed documents – and also for email messages. The corporate letterhead appears as follows.

HAYWOOD DISTRIBUTORS

Industrial Estate
Haywood
HY4 2SK

Every email must be 'signed off' with a standard block of text called a 'signature block', which is inserted automatically by the email software:

[Sender's Name]
[Sender's Position]

Haywood Distributors
Industrial Estate, Haywood, HY4 2SK

Tel: +44 (0)20x xxx xxxx * Fax: +44 (0)20x xxx xxxx *
Web: www.haywooddistributors.co.uk

This message and any attachments are confidential and may contain information that is subject to copyright. If you are not the intended recipient, please notify us immediately by replying to this message and then delete it from your system. While we take reasonable precautions to prevent computer viruses, we cannot accept responsibility for viruses transmitted to your computer and it is your responsibility to make all necessary checks. We may monitor email traffic data and the content of emails to ensure efficient operation of our business, for security, for staff training and for other administrative purposes.

Using templates and house style benefits the organisation both internally and externally.

Internal benefits

Templates make it easier for staff to do their job as they produce standard documents routinely which is easier than creating them separately.

House style reinforces the organisation's ethos and core values.

External benefits

Templates make standard business documents recognisable and therefore they can be processed easily.

House style makes less standard business documents identifiable with a particular organisation which also helps them to be processed easily.

House style reinforces the organisation's ethos and core values which helps to remind customers and suppliers why they trade with that organisation and feel confident that they are right to do so.

ASK 2 Organisations use templates because they support the corporate image.

True ☐

False ☐

Organisations use a 'house style' for documents because companies are required to do so by law.

True ☐

False ☐

3 Creating business documents

When communicating with stakeholders, it is important that the organisation presents a **positive, professional image**.

A key way of presenting that image is by using acceptable business English.

Not slang   Not 'text speak'   Not abbreviated language

How it works

The following is a message you might send a friend via a text message:

RU busy tomoro?

This is not acceptable business English. It uses abbreviations and misspelling, and could be misunderstood. In acceptable business English, the sentence would read:

Are you busy tomorrow?

As you can see, the abbreviations have been changed to full words.

KEYWORD

Slang is very informal language, that is acceptable in some daily speech and informal written communication but not in business communication.

How it works

Examples of common slang that would be inappropriate in business communication are:

Slang	Preferable formal English
Hi	Hello
Cheers	Thank you

There are also some rules about each specific type of communication that you must learn.

For example, for **letter** writing you must learn the correct forms, for example, the beginning and end of the letter.

Salutation	Complimentary close	Context
Dear Sir/Madam/Sirs (name not used)	Yours faithfully	Formal situations Recipients not known
Dear Dr/Mr/Mrs/Ms Bloggs (formal name used)	Yours sincerely	Established relationships Friendly but respectful (eg with superiors, customers, suppliers)
Dear Joe/Josephine	Yours sincerely Kind regards	More personal, informal relationships (eg with colleagues)

Check that for any **letter** you put together, you have included:

- The name and address of the recipient
- Date
- Greeting (or 'salutation' as shown above)
- Subject heading (a brief, helpful 'cue' to what the letter is about)
- The main body of the letter
- Sign-off
- Complimentary close
- Signature. If an assistant is signing a letter on behalf of the writer, the writer's name must be preceded by 'For' (or its equivalent from legal terminology 'pp')

For **emails, memos and reports**, you must ensure they show who they are 'To' and 'From', that they contain the date, and that they have a subject in the subject line.

All forms of communication should include an introduction, the main content, and then a short conclusion.

In the assessment, you will be given a number of options to drag and drop to create a business communication. You will have to choose how many to use and where to put them. The best way to learn this is to see an example and then practise as many questions as you can.

How it works

- You work for ABC Suppliers.
- You have been asked to write a letter to a customer, Linda Thomson, at Greenleys, 21 Hythe Road, Kinsington, KT2 4DR.
- You are to return a cheque received this morning, 26 April 20XX.
- The cheque is in payment of invoice 705 for £195.00.
- Your organisation's name was completed incorrectly on the cheque so it has to be returned for a new one to be issued.
- You have a good relationship with ABC Suppliers who always pay on time.

Using the items below, compose an appropriate letter. You will not need to use all of the items.

There are various options given below. You will need to analyse these to decide which are the right ones to use in the letter. The options have been annotated below to illustrate that process of analysis.

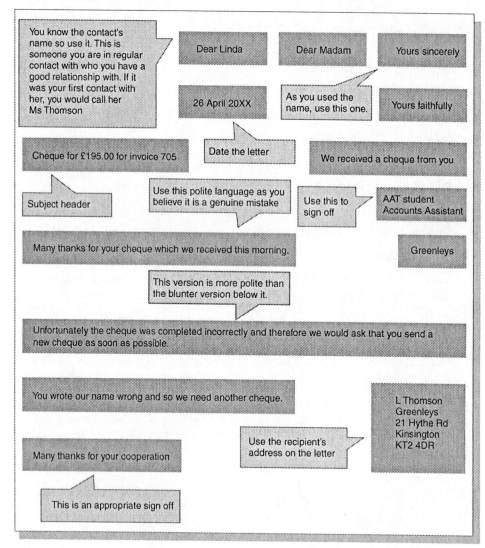

When you have analysed all the options, compile the letter using the appropriate options:

L Thomson
Greenleys
21 Hythe Rd
Kinsington
KT2 4DR

Dear Linda   26 April 20XX

Cheque for £195.00 for invoice 705

Many thanks for your cheque which we received this morning.

Unfortunately the cheque was addressed incorrectly and therefore we would ask that you send a new cheque as soon as possible.

Many thanks for your cooperation

Yours sincerely

AAT student
Accounts Assistant

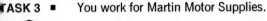

TASK 3

- You work for Martin Motor Supplies.

- You have been asked to write a letter to a potential supplier, Pristine Parts Ltd, at Unit 12, Hurst Industrial Park, Hurst, HU2 4PY.

- You are to ask if they are able to supply 200 units of part XD before 31 May 20XX.

- You have not dealt with Pristine Parts Ltd before, but heard of them at a trade fair.

- The date today is 1 May 20XX.

Using the items below, compose an appropriate letter in the box that follows. You will not need to use all of the items.

| 1 May 20XX | Dear Pristine Parts | Dear Sir | Yours faithfully | Yours sincerely |

| Availability of part XD | AAT student
Accounts Assistant | Head of sales
Pristine Parts Ltd
Unit 12
Hurst Industrial Park
Hurst HU2 4PY |

We are looking for a supplier of the above named part.

Do you have any XDs? We need 200 by 31 May.

Pristine Ltd

Your company was recommended to us at the Hurst Trade Fair in April.

We need to source 200 before 31 May. Would you be able to supply them to us?

Many thanks for your co-operation

If you have the part available we can provide references and would very much like to discuss terms with you.

Solution

You might have to put together or correct other forms of communication. Key things to look for:

- Use of the wrong name

- Spelling errors

- Use of slang

- Blank required elements (such as the subject line in an email, or a lack of recipient's address in a letter)

How it works

Below is an email which has been sent to Clare Short, at Bellfield (bellfield.co.uk). The purpose of the email is to request an annual price list because your organisation, Healy Traders, has not received one as it is accustomed to doing. Errors in the email have been highlighted to illustrate the kind of analysis you need to carry out.

EMAIL

student@healytraders.co.uk

claireshort@bellfield.co.uk

> Clare's name has been misspelt, meaning it is possible that the email won't even arrive.

8 January 20X8

Anual price list

Dear Clare,

> The email contains other spelling mistakes (anual and recieved) which is unprofessional.

I just wanted to enquire if there has been a delay with the price list, as we have not yet recieved it.

Please let me know if we are going to receive a new price list, and when it will arrive if so.

> 'Cheers' is slang, and even in a relatively informal email is unacceptable. 'Many thanks' would be a better complimentary close here, or 'kind regards', which is a complimentary close often used in emails.

Cheers,

Student

As practising putting together appropriate business communications is the best way to learn this skill, here is another task for you to try.

TASK 4   You work for Brown Brothers and have been asked to send an email to David Dunn, your manager, confirming your attendance at annual staff training on 14 and 15 May and requesting overnight accommodation on 14 May.

Using the items at the bottom of the page, compose an appropriate email in the template below.

You will not need to use all of the items.

From: AATstudent@brownbrothers.com

To:

Subject:

---

daviddunn@brownbrothers.com

Confirmation

Annual Staff Training: Confirmation of attendance

Hi David

Please accept this email as confirmation of my attendance at the staff training on 14 and 15 May. As it is over two days I request overnight accommodation on 14 May.

Kind regards
AAT student

danieldune@brownbrother.com

Hello David

I am confirming I want to attend in May and need to stay overnight.

Cheers
AAT student

Chapter overview

Sometimes organisations might have to communicate with their customers and suppliers, or other parties using communication methods other than invoices and statements.

In addition, organisations communicate internally.

Examples of such communications include emails, letters, memos and reports.

Routine business documents (such as invoices, remittance advices) will be sent to customers and suppliers. Other business documents (the letters, emails and reports discussed above) may be sent to other parties associated with the business, known as stakeholders.

Using templates and house style benefits the organisation both internally and externally. Templates make it easier for staff to do their job as they produce standard documents routinely which is easier than creating each one separately.

House style reinforces the organisation's ethos and core values.

Templates make standard business documents recognisable and therefore they can be processed easily.

House style makes less standard business documents identifiable with a particular organisation which also helps them to be processed easily.

House style reinforces the organisation's ethos and core values which helps to remind customers and suppliers why they trade with that organisation and feel confident that they are right to do so.

A key way of presenting a positive, professional image is by using acceptable business English and not slang, text speak or abbreviated language.

You need to learn the forms that govern opening and signing off letters and also the standard contents of letters, emails, memos and reports.

Practising questions designed around putting together business communications is the best way to learn these skills.

Keywords

STAKEHOLDERS are people or groups that have an interest in the organisation.

An **EMAIL** is an electronic form of communication which may be sent both within and outside of the organisation.

A **LETTER** is a written form of communication usually sent outside of the organisation.

A **MEMO** is a relatively informal written form of communication sent from one employee to another within the same organisation.

A **REPORT** is a relatively formal written form of communication which can be sent from one employee to another within the same organisation or outside of the organisation.

A **TEMPLATE** is a standard for business documents, such as invoices and credit notes, so that all such documents issued by a business look the same, and are instantly recognisable for what they are.

'HOUSE STYLE' is an expression of how the organisation wants to present itself in its communications.

SLANG is very informal language that is acceptable in some daily speech and informal written communication, but not in business communication.

Creating business documents:
Test your learning

This chapter gives you question practice on the topics you have covered in the previous chapter. The questions are in the same style you can expect in your assessment. You can find the answers at the back of this Workbook.

1   Organisations communicate using different styles and formats.

  (a) **Show whether the following statements are True or False.**

       Organisations use templates to present a positive, consistent view of the organisation.

       True   ☐

       False   ☐

       Organisations use a house style for documents because it helps customers understand their core values.

       True   ☐

       False   ☐

     You have been asked to circulate the monthly results to department heads.

  ✗ (b) **Select the most appropriate form of communication to accompany the monthly results.**

       ☐   Letter

       ☐   Memo

       ☐   Email

2   **Link the description to the appropriate form of communication by drawing a line from each left hand box to the appropriate right hand box.**

| A written form of communication sent from one employee to another within the same organisation. | **Email** |

| A written form of communication usually sent outside of the organisation. | **Letter** |

| An electronic form of communication which may be sent both within and outside of the organisation. | **Report** |

3   You work for ABC Company and have been asked to send an email to Ben Seales, the managing director, enquiring whether the budgets for the year you sent to him were received.

Using the items below, compose an appropriate email in the template below.

You will not need to use all of the items.

| **From:** AATstudent@abccompany.com |
| **To:** |
| **Subject:** |
| |

benseals@abcompany.com		Bundle of documents

Budgets		Hi Ben

| | | Kind regards |
| | | AAT student |

Please could you confirm whether you received the budgets I sent to you yesterday?		Hello Ben

| | | Cheers |
| benseales@abccompany.com | | AAT student |

| | | Thank you |
| Did you get the budgets? | | AAT student |

4
- You work for Total Traders.

- You have been asked to write a letter to a customer, Tom Parker, at Lyme Ltd, High Road, Thwaite, YK2 6PY.

- You are to inform them that payment of an invoice is extremely overdue and the organisation is going to have to hand it over to their debt collectors.

- The related invoice is 16360 for £13,535.

- The letter is to confirm what you have discussed with Tom over the phone.

- If payment is received within 7 days of today's date (6 July 20XX), no further action will be taken.

Using the items below, compose an appropriate letter in the box on the following page. You will not need to use all of the items.

| 6 July 20XX | Dear Mr Parker | Dear Sir | Yours faithfully | Yours sincerely |

| Availability of part XD | AAT student
Accounts Assistant | T Parker
Lyme Ltd
High Road
Thwaite
YK2 6PY |

Overdue payment for invoice 16360

As discussed previously with you on the telephone, the above debt is seriously overdue.

Unfortunately if payment is not received by us within 7 days of the date of this letter, we shall have to hand this matter over to our debt collectors, ABC Collection Ltd.

| If payment is received within 7 days of the date of this letter, no further action will be taken. | You need to pay the above invoice now or we'll send in the debt collectors. |

You still haven't paid us for this invoice.

Total Traders
Stiring Street, Castlebury, DY4 2RC

5   You work for Hamlyn Traders. You have been asked to send a copy of the new internal control handbook to all department heads. You have been asked to send a memo with the handbook, pointing out that the procedures set out in the handbook are binding from 1 April 20XX, and the major changes from the previous edition, which are set out on page 4 of the handbook. The date today is 24 March 20XX.

Using the items below, compose an appropriate memo in the box below. You will not need to use all of the items but may need to use some more than once.

24 March 20XX	Department Heads	Dear Sir	Cheers	Thank you

New internal control manual	AAT student Accounts Assistant

The new handbook is binding from 1 April 20XX.

I draw your attention to the changes from the previous edition, which are set out on page 4 of the handbook.

Please find the new internal control manual accompanying this memo.	This is the new internal control handbook.

Make sure you have read the changes from the previous edition.

Kind regards	Everybody

MEMO

To: _____

From: _____

Date: _____

Subject: _____

---

6   You work for Westfield Traders. You have been asked to send a report to James Fox, head of the sales department, outlining the sales results for the last six months compared to budget. The overall sales were higher than anticipated, but with some variances from what was expected on a month by month basis.

The date today is 5 July 20XX, and the results are for the six months up to 30 June 20XX.

The results are as follows:

Month	Actual sales	Budgeted sales
	£	£
January 20XX	500,093	500,000
February 20XX	560,943	550,000
March 20XX	650,792	600,000
April 20XX	206,933	250,000
May 20XX	240,044	275,000
June 20XX	350,699	300,000
TOTAL SALES IN PERIOD	2,509,504	2,475,000

Using the items below, compose an appropriate report in the box below. You will not need to use all of the items.

Head of Sales Department		AAT Student

Hi Jamie		Kind regards

RESULTS: The overall sales are £34,504 higher than anticipated for the period, but there are significant variances on the month by month budget, significantly in March and April (which may indicate an error in cut off between those months) and June, when sales are significantly more than was predicted.

Conclusion: Overall sales for the period are higher than were budgeted, however, the pattern of those sales was not as was expected.

Recommendations: I would recommend that some further investigations into market factors is undertaken to explore the reasons behind the high level of sales in June and whether we can expect this trend to continue.

Conclusion: Overall sales for the period are lower than were budgeted, however, the pattern of those sales was not as was expected.

REPORT: SALES IN 6 MONTHS TO 30 JUNE 20XX COMPARED TO BUDGET

Month	Actual sales £	Budgeted sales £
January 20XX	500,093	500,000
February 20XX	560,943	550,000
March 20XX	650,792	600,000
April 20XX	206,933	250,000
May 20XX	240,044	275,000
June 20XX	350,699	300,000
TOTAL SALES IN PERIOD	2,509,504	2,475,000

Month	Actual sales £	Budgeted sales £
January 20XX	500,093	500,000
February 20XX	560,943	550,000
March 20XX	650,923	580,000
April 20XX	206,933	250,000
May 20XX	240,044	275,000
June 20XX	350,699	300,000
TOTAL SALES IN PERIOD	2,509,504	2,455,000

INTRODUCTION: The sales for the period show a better result than was budgeted, but there were some surprises in the month by month analysis.

WESTFIELD TRADERS

TO:

FROM:

DATE:

Chapter tasks:
answers

Chapter tasks: answers

Chapter 1

Task 1

Assets	Liabilities
Premises	Bank loan
Inventory	Bank overdraft
Income	**Expenditure**
Sale	Advertising cost
Interest received	Insurance
	Fuel costs
	Salaries

Task 2

Cash sale	Credit sale
Sale of goods when cash is paid on delivery	Sale of goods when payment is made at a date later than delivery
Sale of services when cash is paid on delivery of the service	Sale of services when cash is paid at a date later than the service was provided
Cash purchase	**Credit purchase**
Purchase of goods when payment is made at the same time as delivery of the goods	Purchase of goods when payment is made at a date later than delivery
Purchase of services when payment is made at the same time as the service is provided	Purchase of a service when payment is made at a later date than the service is provided.

Task 3

1   When income exceeds expenditure, an organisation has made a profit. ☑

2   When expenditure exceeds income, an organisation has made a loss. ☑

3   Income less expenses only equals net profit. ☑

4   Income less cost of sales equals net profit. ☑

5

Organisation	Profit	Loss
Organisation A	✓	
Organisation B	✓	

Task 4

1   Gross profit for Organisation A and Organisation B

Organisation A: £120,000 – £45,000 = £75,000

Organisation B: £364,600 – £149,400 = £215,200

2   Net profit for Organisation A and Organisation B

Organisation A: £75,000 – £45,000 = £30,000

Organisation B: £215,200 – £55,780 = £159,420

Task 5

(a)

Date: **21.08.XX**	Date:	MIDWEST	£50 notes	**150.00**
A/C		BANK	£20 notes	**120.00**
3958229			£10 notes	**20.00**
Cash:		Account name	£5 notes	**10.00**
£312.74		**Haywood Distributors**	£2 coins	
Cheques, POs			£1 coins	
£253.89		Paid in by	Other coin	12.74
Total:		**Student**	Total cash	312.74
£566.63		26-33-20	Cheques, POs	253.89
006924		3958229	Total £	566.63

(b)

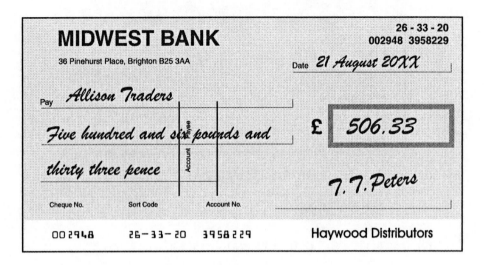

Task 6

1   The following document is entered into the sales day book.

    Sales invoice   ✓

2   An organisation will enter a cheque sent to a supplier into

    Cash payments book   ✓

Chapter 3

Task 1

1

Delivery vehicles	Motor fuel expense
	£
Vehicle 1	128.42
Vehicle 2	196.55
Vehicle 3	86.09
Vehicle 4	112.42
Total	**523.48**

2

Stationery items	Expense
	£
Ink tanks	37.50
Printer paper	18.39
Envelopes	40.91
Pens	7.23
Total	**104.03**

3   (a)   Gross profit = £220,000 – £149,000

£ 71,000

(b)   Net profit = £71,000 – £26,800 – £14,600 – £19,100

£ 10,500

4   (a)   Gross profit = £534,000 – £302,000

£ 232,000

(b)   Net profit = £232,000 – £116,300 – £52,700 – £25,620

£ 37,380

Task 2

The total cost of the hand soap = 12 × £1.25

£ 15

The unit price of a towel = £52.56 ÷ 12

£ 4.38

Task 3

The ratio of the total cost for light and heat to the cost for heat

3:1

Task 4

The proportion of the total cost made up by tea is $\dfrac{150}{750} \div \dfrac{150}{150}$

Task 5

(a) Gross profit as a percentage of sales = £63,425 ÷ £253,700 × 100

| 25 | % |

(b) The increase in the selling price = £569 ÷ 100 × 3

£ | 17.07 |

Task 6

(a) The increase in the selling price = £49 × 1 ÷ 7

£ | 7 |

(b) The increase in the selling price = £25 × 2 ÷ 5

£ | 10 |

Task 7

The average number of miles driven by the delivery vehicles 4,575 ÷ 3

| 1,525 | miles

Chapter 5

Task 1

Limited companies aim to make a **profit**

The National Health Service does not exist to make a **profit**

Task 2

1   Customers of the organisation
    Suppliers of the organisation
    Other departments of the organisation

2   The accounting function provides **information** to other departments in the organisation. This should be **complete, accurate** and timely to ensure that managers in the organisation can make better business decisions.

Task 3

THREE from:

- Keeping confidential files locked up
- Not leaving work on your desk when you leave your desk, even for a few moments
- Password protecting computer files
- Locking your computer screen when you leave your desk, even for a few moments
- Careful disposal of documentation once it is no longer required to be kept
- Giving staff working on sensitive issues private offices

Task 4

Accountants must keep training throughout their careers, to keep up to date with changes in accounting during their career.

True

Task 5

The following are sensible social and environmental policies for an organisation to adopt.

- Don't waste electricity

- Don't buy fuel inefficient vehicles

- Don't leave lights on in unoccupied premises

Task 6

John has seen Rashid smoking in the stationery cupboard. He [should] report this to his supervisor.

Karen is visiting Total Traders. Total Traders [does] have a duty to ensure Karen is safe during her visit.

Amandeep has asked maintenance to increase the number of electric points at her desk. They have not yet done so. Amandeep [should not] use an adaptor brought in from home to enable her to use all her electronic equipment at the same time.

Task 7

The following three statements are true.

- A member of the accounting function should keep a tidy desk to ensure efficient working practices.
- A member of the accounting function should communicate with the team about meeting deadlines.
- A member of the accounting function should communicate with the team to contribute to their work efficiency.

Task 8

Go to your colleague and ask her if there is anything you could do to help her meet her deadline.

Task 9

A person training in an accounting function [should] discuss training needs with their supervisor.

A person who wants a job in an accounting function should be [punctual] .

Chapter 7

Task 1

1   A written form of communication usually sent outside of the organisation is

A letter

2   John has been asked to check that everyone in the sales department is able to attend an important meeting on 25 February 20XX. It is 23 February now. The most appropriate method of communication for him to use is

An email

Task 2

Organisations use templates because they support the corporate image.

True

Organisations use a 'house style' for documents because companies are required to do so by law.

False

Task 3

Head of sales
Pristine Parts Ltd
Unit 12
Hurst Industrial Park
Hurst HU2 4PY

1 May 20XX

Dear Sir

Availability of part XD

Your company was recommended to us at the Hurst Trade Fair in April.

We are looking for a supplier of the above named part.

We need to source 200 before 31 May. Would you be able to supply them to us?

If you have the part available we can provide references and would very much like to discuss terms with you.

Yours faithfully

AAT student
Accounts Assistant

Task 4

From:	AATstudent@brownbrothers.com
To:	daviddunn@brownbrothers.com
Subject:	Annual Staff Training: Confirmation of attendance

Hello David

Please accept this email as confirmation of my attendance at the staff training on 14 and 15 May. As it is over two days I request overnight accommodation on 14 May.

Kind regards
AAT student

Test your learning:
answers

Test your learning: answers

Chapter 2

1 Organisations have assets, liabilities, income and expenditure.

   (a)

Description	Term described
An item spent by the company.	Expenditure
An item earned by the company.	Income

   (b)

Description	Term described
An amount paid to purchase motor insurance.	Expenditure
A cash sale.	Income

2 When an organisation sells goods to a customer and the customer pays for the goods three weeks after the goods are delivered, this is known as **a credit sale**.

   When an organisation buys services from a person and pays that person on the day the service is carried out, this is known as **a cash purchase**.

3 An organisation gives **a receipt** to a customer for goods bought for cash.

   An organisation receives **a credit note** from a supplier listing items returned to the supplier and showing the amount refunded.

   An organisation receives **a purchase order** from a customer requesting that the goods specified in the document be sold to the customer.

4   (a)   A cheque received from a customer   ☑

(b)   Invoice number SI9933 sent by AB Supplies   ☑

(c)

Weaver Traders

Unit 12, Industrial Park, Beeding, OS17 9DP

VAT registration: 427 4234 00

Invoice number: WT00943   24 March 20XX

To: Tharango Ltd

	£
8 items of product SS2 @ £3.60 each	28.80
VAT @ 20%	5.76
TOTAL	34.56

Book of prime entry | **Sales day book** |

Gillespie Enterprises

35 High Road, Steeding ST2 9RT

VAT Registration No: 123 4433 00

INVOICE NUMBER: 3546

INVOICE DATE: 6 March 20XX

To: Weaver Traders, Unit 12, Industrial Park, Beeding

	£
4 items of product XX @ £0.99 each	3.96
VAT @ 20%	0.79
Total	4.75

Book of prime entry | **Purchases day book** |

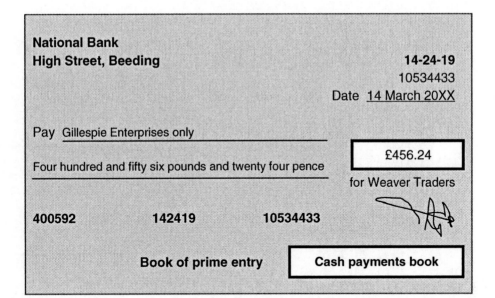

National Bank
High Street, Beeding   14-24-19
                                                                        10534433
                                                        Date 14 March 20XX

Pay Gillespie Enterprises only

Four hundred and fifty six pounds and twenty four pence   £456.24

                                                        for Weaver Traders

400592   142419   10534433

              Book of prime entry   **Cash payments book**

5   In an alphanumerical coding system the code must consist of numbers followed by
     letters.

     False   The code can be letters followed by numbers.

6   Purchase invoices can be entered into the system together.

     True   ✓

7   (a)   17 April 20XX

     (b)   £150

     (c)   £309.35

     (d)   A paying-in slip should be signed and dated by the person who is paying in
           the money.

           True

8

National Bank	
National Bank Business Centre, Main Road	**14-88-51**
	44830113
	Date 16 April 20XY

Pay   DK Traders

Sixty four pounds and eighty seven pence only

£64.87

for Hollands Traders

100346   **148851**   **44830113**

National Bank	
National Bank Business Centre, Main Road	**14-88-51**
	44830113
	Date 16 April 20XY

Pay   SG Company

Four hundred and sixty four pounds and

£464.82

eighty two pence only

for Hollands Traders

100347   **148851**   **44830113**

9   (a)   Income less cost of sales equals gross profit.

True   ☑

(b)   (i)   Gross profit = £377,800 – £184,900

£ | 192,900 |

(ii)   Net profit = £192,900 – £94,500

£ | 98,400 |

Chapter 4

1   (a)   The average price of each car = £958.30 ÷ 2

£ | 479.15 |

(b) | **Cash transaction** |

2   (a)   (i)   Gross profit = £577,500 – £285,900

£ | 291,600 |

(ii)   Net profit = £291,600 – £197,583

£ | 94,017 |

(b)   Net profit as a percentage of sales = £94,017 ÷ £577,500 × 100

| 16.28 | %

3   (a)   The increase in selling price for product number 52 = £17 × 1 ÷ 5

£ | 3.40 |

(b)   The increase in selling price for product number 12 = £18 ÷ 100 × 6

£ | 1.08 |

4   (a)   The increase in selling price for product number 104 = £62 × 1 ÷ 8

£ | 7.75 |

(b)   The increase in selling price for product number AZ25 = £9 ÷ 100 × 6

£ | 0.54 |

5 (a) Sales at Outlet 4

Sales per outlet	£
Outlet 1	250,368.25
Outlet 2	199,473.79
Outlet 3	302,699.39
Outlet 4	375,210.17
Total	1,127,751.60

(b) Average sales per outlet = 1,127,751.60 ÷ 4

£ 281,937.90

(c) Sales from menswear

Item	£
Menswear	76,203
Ladieswear	61,506
Childrenswear	62,595
Household fabrics	50,076
Total	250,380

(d) The ratio of total sales at Outlet 1 to sales of childrenswear at Outlet 1

4:1

(e) The proportion that household fabrics is of the total sales at Outlet 1

$\frac{1}{5}$

Working

$$\frac{50,076}{250,380} \div \frac{50,076}{50,076} = \frac{1}{5}$$

6   (a)   The costs at Premises 2

Costs per premises	£
Premises 1	50,924.72
Premises 2	51,125.22
Total	102,049.94

(b)   Average cost per premises = 102,049.94 ÷ 2

£   51,024.97

(c)   The ratio of total costs to administration costs

5:1

Chapter 6

1   (a)   A sole trader is a   **private sector**   organisation.

(b)   The police service   **does not**   aim to make a profit.

2   (a)   Detailed expenditure analysis provided by the accounting department is used by the general public to make business decisions.

False   ✓

(b)   An example of a customer of the accounting department is the organisation's suppliers.

True   ✓

3   Information about pay increases held on the computer should be kept **in a password protected file with access restricted to those who need the information.**

A supplier of the organisation where you work asks you who the main customers of the organisation are. You reply: '**I am sorry but I cannot give you any information as it is confidential'.**

4   Accountants should behave with integrity in all circumstances.

True   ✓

✗ Organisations can behave in a socially irresponsible manner because they have no responsibility to the general public.

False   ✓

5   Organisations should observe health and safety guidelines.

(a)   An organisation   **must**   provide a safe environment for

anyone on the premises

(b)   An employee has a duty not to put him or herself in danger at work.

True   ✓

It is important to keep a tidy desk to ensure you work efficiently.

True   ✓

6   It is important to understand the skills and attributes needed by a finance professional.

(a)   A finance professional should   **communicate well**   and be   **reliable**

(b)   Training for the AAT qualification is the only appropriate method of formal training for a finance professional.

False   ✓

One reason somebody training to be a finance professional discusses training needs with their supervisor is so that the supervisor can make recommendations.

True   ✓

7   It is important to work effectively. You should take the following action.

(a)   ✓   Ask your colleague if she is able to spare any time to help you meet the deadline.

(b)   Planning is very important to help you meet your deadlines. The following document is a planning aid.

✓   Schedule

Chapter 8

1   (a)   Organisations use templates to present a positive, consistent view of the organisation.

   True

   Organisations use a house style for documents because it helps customers understand their core values.

   True

   (b)   The most appropriate form of communication to accompany the monthly results.

             Memo

2

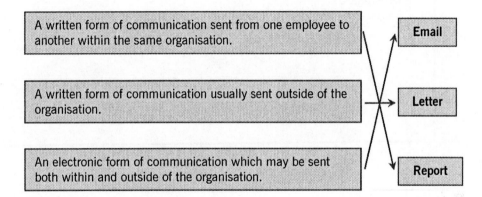

3

From:	AATstudent@abccompany.com
To:	benseales@abccompany.com
Subject:	Budgets

Hello Ben

Please could you confirm whether you received the budgets I sent to you yesterday?

Kind regards
AAT student

4

Total Traders
Stiring Street, Castlebury, DY4 2RC

T Parker
Lyme Ltd
High Road
Thwaite
YK2 6PY

6 July 20XX

Dear Mr Parker

Overdue payment for invoice 16360

As discussed previously with you on the telephone, the above debt is seriously overdue.

Unfortunately if payment is not received by us within 7 days of the date of this letter, we shall have to hand this matter over to our debt collectors, ABC Collection Ltd.

If payment is received within 7 days of the date of this letter, no further action will be taken.

Yours sincerely

AAT student
Accounts Assistant

5

> **MEMO**
>
> **To:** Department Heads
>
> **From:** AAT student, Accounts Assistant
>
> **Date:** 24 March 20XX
>
> **Subject** New internal control manual
>
> ---
>
> Please find the new internal control manual accompanying this memo.
>
> I draw your attention to the changes from the previous edition, which are set out on page 4 of the handbook.
>
> The new handbook is binding from 1 April 20XX.
>
> Thank you

6

WESTFIELD TRADERS

REPORT: SALES IN 6 MONTHS TO 30 JUNE 20XX COMPARED TO BUDGET

TO: Head of Sales Department

FROM: AAT Student

DATE: 5 July 20XX

INTRODUCTION: The sales for the period show a better result than was budgeted, but there were some surprises in the month by month analysis.

RESULTS: The overall sales are £34,504 higher than anticipated for the period, but there are significant variances on the month by month budget, significantly in March and April (which may indicate an error in cut off between those months) and June, when sales are significantly more than was predicted.

Month	Actual sales £	Budgeted sales £
January 20XX	500,093	500,000
February 20XX	560,943	550,000
March 20XX	650,792	600,000
April 20XX	206,933	250,000
May 20XX	240,044	275,000
June 20XX	350,699	300,000
TOTAL SALES IN PERIOD	2,509,504	2,475,000

Conclusion: Overall sales for the period are higher than were budgeted, however, the pattern of those sales was not as was expected.

Recommendations: I would recommend that some further investigations into market factors is undertaken to explore the reasons behind the high level of sales in June and whether we can expect this trend to continue.

BPP
LEARNING MEDIA

Practice assessments

AAT sample assessment 1

1.1 Organisations have assets, liabilities, income and expenditure.

(a) **Which of the following statements describes an asset? Place a tick (✓) in the appropriate box.**

An asset is something an organisation owes. ☐

An asset is something an organisation owns. ☐ ✓

An asset is something an organisation earns. ☐

(b) **Place a tick (✓) in the appropriate column of the table below to show whether each of the items listed is an example of an asset, a liability, income or expenditure. You should not place more than one tick against each item.**

Item	Asset	Liability	Income	Expenditure
Sales			✓	
Wages				✓
Machinery	✓			

1.2 It is important to understand the terminology used when buying and selling goods for cash and on credit.

Insert an item from the following list into the right hand column of the table below to identify the term described. You will not need to use all of the items.

- Cash sales
- Cash purchases
- Credit sales
- Credit purchases
- A debtor
- A creditor

Description	Term described
A transaction to purchase goods when payment is made immediately.	
Someone who owes money to an organisation for goods sold by the organisation.	

1.3   Your organisation purchased 24 boxes of printer paper at £4.65 per box from Brookes Stationers.

(a)   **What is the total cost of the printer paper?**

£ [111.60]

Brookes Stationers agreed to issue an invoice asking your organisation to pay for the printer paper within 30 days.

(b)   **Is the purchase of the printer paper:**

(i)   A cash transaction; or

(ii)   A credit transaction?

[   ]

1.4   Organisations issue and receive different documents when buying and selling goods.

Complete the sentences below by inserting the most appropriate option from the following list:

- a purchases order
- a receipt
- an invoice
- a statement of account

An organisation sends [   ] to request payment from a customer who has bought goods on credit.

An organisation issues [   ] to a customer who has paid for goods in cash.

An organisation sends [   ] to a supplier detailing the goods it wants to buy.

1.5   You work for Latif Traders. You are preparing to record some documents in the books of prime entry.

(a)   **Select which ONE of the documents below will be entered in the purchases returns day-book.**

An invoice sent by a supplier.   ☐

A credit note sent by a supplier.   ☐

A cheque sent to a supplier.   ☐

✂(b) **Select which ONE of the documents below will be entered in the cash receipts book.**

A cash payments listing.　　☐

A cheque sent by a customer.　　☐

A cheque sent to a supplier.　　☐

(c) **Insert an item from the following list into the bottom right hand box of each document to show which book of prime entry that document will be entered into. You will not need to use all of the items.**

- Cash payments book
- Cash receipts book
- Purchases day-book
- Purchases returns day-book
- Sales day-book
- Sales returns day-book

Pebbles Printing
5 Valley Road, Redport, RE7 9PP
VAT Registration No. 217 8621 00

Invoice No. 249

To: Latif Traders　　　　　　　　　　　　　　21 July 20XX
24 Lower Street,
Redport, RE4 7GD

	£
80 catalogues @ £1.40 each	112.00
VAT @ 20%	22.40
Total	134.40

Terms: 30 days net　**Book of prime entry**　　☐

Latif Traders

24 Lower Street, Redport, RE4 7GD
VAT Registration No. 456 7421 00

Credit note No. 28

To: GBH Ltd   24 July 20XX
47 Bissel Street,
Redport, RE6 8FR

	£
4 items of product XYZ @ £6 each	24.00
VAT @ 20%	4.80
Total	28.80

Terms: 30 days net   **Book of prime entry**

Latif Traders

Cheques to suppliers listing

25 July 20XX

	£
F Adams and Co	200.00
HR Electrics	65.90
Total	265.90

Book of prime entry

1.6 Some organisations use coding within the accounting records.

Show whether the following statement is True or False.

In an alphabetical coding system all codes consist of letters and numbers.

True ☐

False ☐

1.7 Your organisation uses a batch processing system to enter purchases invoices into the accounting records.

Show whether the following statement is True or False.

✶ In a batch processing system, purchases invoices are entered into the accounting records as soon as they are received.

True ☐

False ☐

1.8 On 24 July 20XX you have been asked to pay the following items into Bond Ltd's bank account:

- Two × £20 notes
- Five × £5 notes
- Six × £2 coins
- Eight × 10p coins
- One × cheque for £350.60

(a) **Complete the paying-in slip below. Make sure you enter all the figures in pounds and pence, for example 16.00, 2.50 and 0.75.**

Date:	City Bank plc Redport	£50 notes	
		£20 notes	
		£10 notes	
	Account: Bond Ltd	£5 notes	
		£2 coins	
		£1 coins	
	Paid in by: AAT student	Other coin	
		Total cash	
	30-45-22 10678465	Cheques, POs	
		Total £	

(b) **Show whether the following statement is True or False.**

Paying-in slips should be signed by the person who pays the items into the bank.

True ☐

False ☐

1.9 It is important to ensure cheques sent to suppliers are completed properly.

On 17 July 20XX you are preparing a cheque for £178.90 to send to a supplier, Dawsons Electrics.

(a) **Which ONE of the following options shows the date as it should be written on the cheque?**

July 20XX ☐

17 July 20XX ☐

17 July ☐

(b) **Which ONE of the following options shows the payee as it should be written on the cheque?**

Supplier ☐

Dewson ☐

Dawsons Electrics ☐

(c) **Which ONE of the following options shows the amount in words as it should be written on the cheque?**

Seventeen hundred and eight pounds and ninety pence ☐

One hundred and seventy eight pounds and ninety pence ☐

Seventeen pounds and eighty nine pence ☐

(d) **Show whether the following statement is True or False.**

If the amount in words on a cheque is different from the amount in figures the cheque is still correct.

True ☐

False ☐

1.10 At the end of every year your organisation calculates the profit or loss for the year.

(a) **Complete the sentence below by selecting the most appropriate option from the following list.**

- equals
- is more than
- is less than

When income [   ] expenditure this results in a profit.

Last year your organisation recorded income and expenditure as shown in the table below:

Income and expenditure	£
Sales	120,000
Cost of sales	72,000
Wages	16,200
Office expenses	14,400
Selling expenses	9,880

40480

(b) **Use the income and expenditure figures to complete the following calculations.**

(i) **Calculate gross profit**

£ [   ]

(ii) **Calculate net profit**

£ [   ]

(c) **Use your answer from (b)(i) to calculate gross profit as a percentage of sales. If it is appropriate make sure you give your answer to 2 decimal places.**

[   ] %

1.11 An organisation is reviewing the selling price of some of its products.

The current selling price of product number 256 is £24.00. This is to be increased by 6%.

(a) **Calculate the increase in selling price for product number 256.**

£ [   ]

The current selling price of product number 347 is £18.00. This is to be increased by 1/8 (one eighth).

(b) **Calculate the increase in selling price for product number 347.**

£ [   ]

If necessary, you may use the space below for your workings.

1.12 Your organisation keeps detailed records of expenses.

Motor fuel expenses for each of four delivery vehicles are shown in the table below.

(a) **Complete the table to show the total expense for motor fuel.**

Delivery vehicles	Motor fuel expense
	£
Vehicle 1	100.68
Vehicle 2	96.45
Vehicle 3	88.76
Vehicle 4	103.83
Total	

(b) **Calculate the average motor fuel expense per vehicle.**

£ [   ]

Expenses relating to items of stationery are shown in the table below.

(c) **Complete the table to show the expense for envelopes.**

Stationery items	Expense
	£
Ink tanks	25.00
Printer paper	23.90
Envelopes	59.60
Pens	11.60
Total	75.00

(d)   **Which of the following is the ratio of the total expense for stationery items to the expense for ink tanks?**

- 2:1
- 3:1
- 4:1

2.1   There are different types of organisation.

Complete the following sentences by selecting the most appropriate option from the list of items below each sentence.

The National Health Service is a

organisation.

- private sector
- public sector
- charitable

A charity aim to make a profit.

- does
- does not

2.2   It is important to understand the role of the accounting department within an organisation.

Show whether the following statements are True or False.

Information provided by the accounting department is used by managers within the organisation to make better business decisions.

True

False

An example of a customer of the accounting department is people living close to the organisation.

True

False

2.3   You work for Orchard Fruits and have been asked to send an email to Sarah Clarke, your manager, confirming your attendance at annual staff training on 10 and 11 July and requesting overnight accommodation on 10 July.

Using the items at the bottom of the page, compose an appropriate email in the template below. You will not need to use all of the items.

From:	AATstudent@orchard.com
To:	
Subject:	

Susieclare@orchard.com

Confirmation

② Annual Staff Training: Confirmation of attendance

Hi Susie

4. Please accept this email as confirmation of my attendance at the staff training on 10 and 11 July. As it is over two days I request overnight accommodation on 10 July.

5 Kind regards
AAT student

() Sarahclarke@orchard.com

3 Hello Sarah

I am confirming I want to attend in July and need to stay overnight.

Cheers
AAT student

BPP
LEARNING MEDIA

2.4 Organisations communicate using different styles and formats.

(a) **Show whether the following statements are True or False.**

Organisations use templates because they have to be used by law.

True   ☐

False   ☐

Organisations use a 'house style' for documents because it supports the corporate image.

True   ☐

False   ☐

You have been asked to send a price list to a customer.

(b) **Select the most appropriate form of communication to accompany the price list.**

☐   Letter

☐   Memo

☐   Report

2.5 It is important to observe confidentiality.

Complete the following sentences by inserting the most appropriate option from the list below each sentence.

Information about staff wages held on the computer should be kept

- in an area where all employees have access.
- in a password protected file with access restricted to those who need the information.

Your sister is a customer of the organisation where you work. She asks you how much profit the organisation is making. You reply:

- 'I am sorry but I cannot give you any information as it is confidential'.
- 'As you are a customer I can tell you that they made £1 million profit'.

BPP
LEARNING MEDIA

2.6 Finance professionals and organisations have a duty to behave in a professional and socially responsible manner.

Complete each sentence in the following table by inserting the most appropriate item from the list below. You will not need to use all of the options.

Sentence	Item
Once accountants are qualified...	
An accountant should always...	
An organisation should adopt socially responsible practices because...	
An example of an socially responsible policy is to ...	

- they do not need to complete any further training.
- they should complete sufficient training to maintain professional competence.
- behave with honesty and integrity.
- have monthly staff parties.
- it has a duty to act ethically.
- ensure lights are switched off when the offices are closed.

2.7 Organisations should observe health and safety guidelines.

(a) **Complete this sentence by inserting the most appropriate option from the list below each box.**

An organisation [ ] to provide a safe environment for [ ]

has a duty   staff only.
has a choice whether   visitors only.
does not have   staff and visitors.

(b) **Show whether the following statements are True or False.**

An employee has a duty to report all hazards to a manager.

True [ ]

False [ ]

A tidy desk will encourage you to work more efficiently.

True [ ]

False [ ]

2.8 It is important to understand the skills and attributes needed by a finance professional.

(a) **Complete this sentence by inserting the most appropriate option from the list next to each box.**

A finance professional should [   ]   have good communication skills
have good creative skills

and be able to show a [   ]   professional attitude.
casual attitude.

(b) **Show whether the following statements are True or False.**

A finance professional can acquire knowledge by attending a training course.

True ☐

False ☐

It is important for somebody who is currently training to be a finance professional to meet regularly with their manager to discuss their specific training needs.

True ☐

False ☐

2.9 It is important to work effectively.

(a) **Answer the following questions by selecting the most appropriate option.**

It is Friday lunchtime and you have completed all of your tasks for the week. Your colleague has just received a report. The report is late and she is very busy with other work. Consequently it is unlikely she will be able to complete all of her tasks.

Which ONE of the following actions should you take?

☐ Start tidying your desk to make sure it is clear for next week.

☐ Go to your colleague and ask her if there is anything you could do to help her.

☐ Go home early.

Planning is very important to help you meet your deadlines.

Which ONE of the following documents below is a planning aid?

☐   Expenses sheet.

☐   To do list.

☐   Holiday request form.

It is important to use an appropriate form of communication at all times.

(b) **Link the description to the appropriate form of communication by drawing a line from each left hand box to the appropriate right hand box.**

An electronic form of communication which may be sent both within and outside of the organisation.	Letter
A written form of communication sent from one employee to another within the same organisation.	Email
A written form of communication usually sent outside of the organisation.	Memo

2.10

- You work for Samuel Motors.

- You have been asked to write a letter to a customer, Sandra Robinson, at Ashdowns, Fylde Road, Mythop. FY6 2DP.

- You are to return a cheque received this morning, 6 July 20XX.

- The cheque is in payment of invoice 236 for £35.00.

- The cheque was dated incorrectly and will have to be returned for a new one to be issued.

- You have a good relationship with Ashdowns who always pay on time.

Using the items below, compose an appropriate letter in the box on the next page. You will not need to use all of the items.

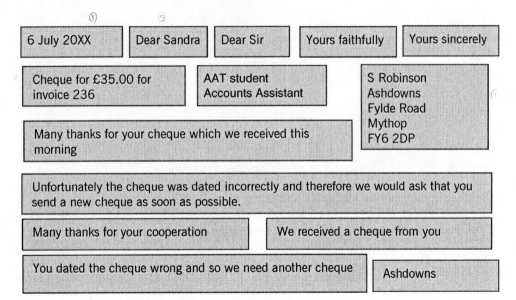

| 6 July 20XX | Dear Sandra | Dear Sir | Yours faithfully | Yours sincerely |

| Cheque for £35.00 for invoice 236 | AAT student | Accounts Assistant | S Robinson Ashdowns Fylde Road Mythop FY6 2DP |

Many thanks for your cheque which we received this morning

Unfortunately the cheque was dated incorrectly and therefore we would ask that you send a new cheque as soon as possible.

| Many thanks for your cooperation | We received a cheque from you |

| You dated the cheque wrong and so we need another cheque | Ashdowns |

Samuel Motors
Back Henry Street, Thornbury, FY7 1XY

AAT sample assessment 1: answers

1.1

(a) An asset is something an organisation owns.

(b)

Item	Asset	Liability	Income	Expenditure
Sales			✓	
Wages				✓
Machinery	✓			

1.2

Description	Term described
A transaction to purchase goods when payment is made immediately.	Cash purchase
Someone who owes money to an organisation for goods sold by the organisation.	A debtor

1.3

(a) £ | 111.60 |

(b) | **Credit transaction** |

1.4

An organisation sends **an invoice** to request payment from a customer who has bought goods on credit.

An organisation issues **a receipt** to a customer who has paid for goods in cash.

An organisation sends **a purchases order** to a supplier detailing the goods it wants to buy.

1.5

    (a)   A credit note sent by a supplier   ☑

    (b)   A cheque sent by a customer   ☑

    (c)

Pebbles Printing

5 Valley Road, Redport, RE7 9PP

VAT Registration No. 217 8621 00

Invoice No. 249

To: Latif Traders   21 July 20XX
      24 Lower Street,
      Redport, RE4 7GD

	£
80 catalogues @ £1.40 each	112.00
VAT @ 20%	22.40
Total	134.40

Terms: 30 days net   **Book of prime entry:**   **Purchases day-book**

Latif Traders

24 Lower Street, Redport, RE4 7GD
VAT Registration No. 456 7421 00

Credit note No. 28

To: GBH Ltd   24 July 20XX
     Bissel Street,
     Redport, RE6 8FR

	£
4 items of product XYZ @ £6 each	24.00
VAT @ 20%	4.80
Total	28.80

Terms: 30 days net   **Book of prime entry:** | **Sales returns day-book** |

Latif Traders

Cheques to suppliers listing

25 July 20XX

	£
F Adams and Co	200.00
HR Electrics	65.90
Total	265.90

Book of prime entry: | **Cash payments book** |

1.6 In an alphabetical coding system all codes consist of letters and numbers.

False

1.7 In a batch processing system, purchases invoices are entered into the accounting records as soon as they are received.

False   ☑

1.8

(a)

Date: 24 July 20XX	City Bank plc Redport	£50 notes	
		£20 notes	40.00
		£10 notes	
	Account:	£5 notes	25.00
	Bond Ltd	£2 coins	12.00
		£1 coins	
	Paid in by	Other coin	0.80
	AAT Student	Total cash	77.80
	30-45-22 10678465	Cheques, POs	350.60
		Total £	428.40

(b) Paying-in slips should be signed by the person who pays the items into the bank.

True   ☑

1.9

(a) 17 July 20XX

(b) Dawsons Electrics

(c) One hundred and seventy eight pounds and ninety pence

(d) If the amount in words on a cheque is different from the amount in figures the cheque is still correct.

False   ☑

1.10

(a) When income **is more than** expenditure this results in a profit.

(b) (i)   £ 48,000

(ii)   £ 7,520

(c)   40   %

1.11

    (a)   The increase in selling price for product number 256.

         £   **1.44**

    (b)   The increase in selling price for product number 347.

         £   **2.25**

1.12

    (a)

Delivery vehicles	Motor fuel expense
	£
Vehicle 1	100.68
Vehicle 2	96.45
Vehicle 3	88.76
Vehicle 4	103.83
Total	**389.72**

    (b)   The average motor fuel expense per vehicle

         £   **97.43**

    (c)

Stationery items	Expense
	£
Ink tanks	25.00
Printer paper	23.90
Envelopes	14.50
Pens	11.60
Total	**75.00**

    (d)   Ratio of total expense for stationery items to the expense for ink tanks

        3:1

2.1

    The National Health Service is a   **public sector**   organisation.

    A charity   **does not**   aim to make a profit.

2.2 Information provided by the accounting department is used by managers within the organisation to make better business decisions.

True ✓

An example of a customer of the accounting department is people living close to the organisation.

False ✓

2.3

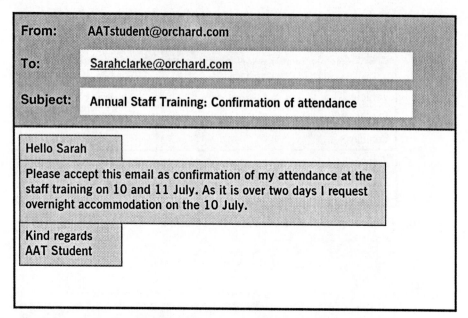

From: AATstudent@orchard.com

To: Sarahclarke@orchard.com

Subject: Annual Staff Training: Confirmation of attendance

Hello Sarah

Please accept this email as confirmation of my attendance at the staff training on 10 and 11 July. As it is over two days I request overnight accommodation on the 10 July.

Kind regards
AAT Student

2.4

(a) Organisations use templates because they have to be used by law.

False ✓

Organisations use a 'house style' for documents because it supports the corporate image.

True ✓

(b) Letter ✓

2.5

Information about staff wages held on the computer should be kept **in a password protected file with access restricted to those who need the information.**

Your sister is a customer of the organisation where you work. She asks you how much profit the organisation is making. You reply: **'I am sorry but I cannot give you any information as it is confidential'.**

2.6

Sentence	Item
Once accountants are qualified...	**... they must complete sufficient training to maintain their professional competence**
An accountant should always...	**... behave with honesty and integrity**
An organisation should adopt socially responsible practices because...	**... it has a duty to act ethically**
An example of a socially responsible policy is to ...	**... ensure lights are switched off when the offices are closed**

2.7

(a) An organisation **has a duty** to provide a safe environment for **staff and visitors**

(b) An employee has a duty to report all hazards to a manager.

   True

   A tidy desk will encourage you to work more efficiently.

   True

2.8

(a) A finance professional should **have good communication skills** and be

   able to show a **professional attitude**

(b) A finance professional can acquire knowledge by attending a training course.

   True

   It is important for somebody who is currently training to be a finance professional to meet regularly with their manager to discuss their specific training needs.

   True

2.9

(a) ☑ Go to your colleague and ask her if there is anything you could do to help her

   ☑ To do list.

(b)

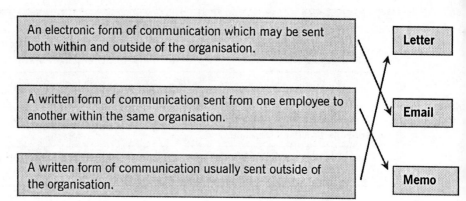

An electronic form of communication which may be sent both within and outside of the organisation.		Letter
A written form of communication sent from one employee to another within the same organisation.		Email
A written form of communication usually sent outside of the organisation.		Memo

2.10

Samuel Motors
Back Henry Street, Thornbury, FY7 1XY

S Robinson
Ashdowns
Fylde Road
Mythop
FY6 2DP

6 July 20XX

Dear Sandra

Cheque for £35.00 for Invoice 236

Many thanks for your cheque which we received this morning.

Unfortunately the cheque was dated incorrectly and therefore we would ask that you send a new cheque as soon as possible.

Yours sincerely,

AAT student
Accounts Assistant

AAT sample assessment 2

1.1 Organisations have assets, liabilities, income and expenditure.

(a) **Complete the following sentences by selecting the most appropriate option.**

is something an organisation owes.

is something an organisation owns.

Options

An asset
A liability
Income
Expenditure

(b) **Place a tick in the appropriate column of the table to show whether each of the items is an example of an asset, a liability, income or expenditure.**

Item	Asset	Liability	Income	Expenditure
Sales				
Electricity				

1.2 It is important to understand the terminology used when buying and selling goods for cash and on credit.

Use the appropriate term to identify the item described.

Description	Term
A transaction to sell goods when payment is made immediately.	
A transaction to purchase services when payment is made a month later.	

List of terms

Cash sales	Credit purchases
Cash purchases	A debtor
Credit sales	A creditor

1.3 Your organisation sold 128 boxes of oranges on credit for £2.62 per box.

(a) **What is the total selling price of the oranges?**

£ [   ]

(b) **When will your organisation receive payment for the oranges?**

[   ]

Before the oranges are sold
At the same time as the oranges are sold
Some time after the oranges are sold

1.4 Organisations issue and receive different documents when buying and selling goods.

Link each document below to the appropriate description by drawing a line from the left hand box to the right hand box.

Document	Description
Sales invoice	A document sent to a creditor accompanying a payment, listing items included in that payment.
Statement of account	A document sent to a customer listing recent transactions and requesting payment of the amount owed by a customer.
Remittance advice	A document sent to a customer listing goods sold and requesting payment.

1.5 You work for Gould Ltd. You are preparing to record some documents in the books of prime entry.

(a) **Select which ONE of the documents below will be entered in the sales day-book.**

An invoice sent to a customer ☐

A credit note sent to a customer ☐

A cheque sent by a customer ☐

(b) **Select which ONE of the documents below will be entered in the cash receipts book.**

A cash payments listing ☐

A cheque sent by a customer ☐

A cheque sent to a supplier ☐

(c)   **Place the appropriate item in each document below to show which book of prime entry that document will be entered into. You will need not to use all of the items.**

Bateman Retail
19 White Lane, Conglefield, WA4 6TX
VAT Registration No. 176 39688 00
Invoice No. 2045

To: Gould Ltd   19 July 20XX
     3 Granby Road,
     Sailport SS1 2HS

                                                         £
80 panels @ £4.35 each   348.00
VAT @ 20%   69.60
                                                    ———
Total   417.60

Terms: 30 days net **Book of prime entry**   [   ]

Gould Ltd
3 Granby Road, Sailport, SS1 2HS
VAT Registration No. 397 3813 00
Credit note No. CN620

To: Mayfield Associates   10 July 20XX
     22 Lystral Lane,
     Fleetbury FY5 2DT

                                                         £
20 items of product AB2 @ £5.70 each   114.00
VAT @ 20%   22.80
                                                    ———
Total   136.80

                     Book of prime entry   [   ]

Gould Ltd
Cash payments listing

20 July 20XX

	£
LH Hallsworth – for repairs to roof	67.00
Express Cars – taxi fare	35.60
Total	102.60

Book of prime entry

List items

Cash payments book
Purchases returns day-book
Cash receipts book
Sales day-book
Purchases day-book
Sales returns day-book

1.6 Some organisations use coding within the accounting records.

An organisation has a code for one of its debtors as 100654.

Which ONE of the following options identifies the type of code used by the organisation for its debtors?

Alphabetical ☐

Numerical ☐

Alphanumerical ☐

1.7 Your organisation uses a batch processing system to enter purchases invoices into the accounting records.

Show whether the following statement is True or False.

In a batch processing system a group of purchases invoices are entered into the accounting records at the same time.

True ☐

False ☐

1.8 On 24 July 20XX you have been asked to pay the following items into Fraser Ltd's bank account.

Three	£50 notes
Five	£10 notes
Six	£1 coins
Eleven	10p coins

One cheque for £270.00

(a) **Enter these items and the date onto the paying in slip below. Make sure you enter all figures in pounds and pence. For example 16.00, 2.50 and 0.75.**

Date:	County Bank plc	£50 notes	
	Northport	£20 notes	
		£10 notes	
	Account	£5 notes	
	Fraser Ltd	£2 coin	
		£1 coin	
	Paid by	Other coin	
		Total cash	
	40-29-67	Cheques, POs	
	10672348	Total £	

(b) **Show whether the following statement is True or False.**

The person who should sign the 'Paid in by' section of the paying in slip should be the bank cashier.

True ☐

False ☐

1.9 It is important to ensure cheques sent to suppliers are completed properly.

On 11 July 20XX you are preparing a cheque for £1,347.09 to send to a supplier, Dawes Paints.

(a) **Which ONE of the following options shows the date as it should be written on the cheque?**

July 20XX ☐

11 July 20XX ☐

1 July 20XX ☐

(b)   **Which ONE of the following options shows the payee as it should be written on the cheque?**

Supplier   ☐

Drawes   ☐

Dawes Paints   ☐

(c)   **Which ONE of the following options shows the amount in words as it should be written on the cheque?**

One thousand three hundred and forty seven pounds and ninety pence   ☐

One thousand three hundred and forty seven pounds and nine pence   ☐

One thousand three hundred and forty seven pounds only   ☐

(d)   **Show whether the following statement is True or False.**

The amount in words on a cheque should match exactly the amount in figures.

True   ☐

False   ☐

1.10 At the end of every year your organisation calculates the profit or loss for the year.

(a)   **Complete the following sentence by selecting the most appropriate option.**

When income [   ] expenditure this results in a profit.

equals
is more than
is less than

Last year your organisation recorded income and expenditure as shown in the table below.

Income and expenditure	£
Sales	260,000
Cost of sales	114,000
Wages	51,810
Office expenses	12,250
Selling expenses	14,340

(b)   **Use the income and expenditure figures to complete the following calculations.**

    (i)   **Calculate gross profit**

      £ [   ]

    (ii)   **Calculate net profit**

      £ [   ]

(c)   **Using your answer from (b)(ii) calculate net profit as a percentage of sales. If your answer is not a whole number make sure you give your answer to 2 decimal places.**

    [   ] %

1.11 An organisation is reviewing the selling price of some of its products.

The current selling price of product number 361 is £24.00. This is to be increased by 15%.

(a)   **Calculate the increase in selling price for product number 361.**

    £ [   ]

The current selling price of product number 256 is £152.00. This is to be increased by ¼ (one quarter).

(b)   **Calculate the increase in selling price for product number 256.**

    £ [   ]

1.12 Your organisation keeps detailed records of sales by region.

Sales for last month are shown in the table below.

(a)   **Complete the table to show the total sales for the last month.**

Region	Sales £
North	5,683.68
South	25,289.02
East	3,672.70
West	2,455.00
Total	

(b) **Calculate the average sales per region for the last month.**

£ [ ]

Your organisation keeps detailed records of expenses by store.

Expenses relating to different stores are shown in the table below.

(c) **Complete the table to show the expenses for store S214.**

Store Code	Expenses £
N001	25,680.00
B010	34,210.90
S214	
J967	6,420.00
Total	109,546.33

(d) **Calculate the ratio of the expenses for store N001 to the expenses for store J967.**

[ ]

2.1 There are different types of organisation.

Place a tick in the appropriate column of the table below to show whether each of the organisations listed are in the public sector, private sector or charitable sector.

Organisation	Public sector	Private sector	Charitable sector
A shop selling goods specifically to raise funds for sick children			
The local police service			

2.2 It is important to understand the role of the accounting department within an organisation.

Show whether the following statements are True or False.

Information produced by the accounting department will only be used by managers in the accounting department.

True [ ]

False [✓]

Customers of the accounting department are always from outside of the organisation.

True ☐

False ☐

2.3 You work for Parry Stores and have been asked to send an email to Mohan Singh, your manager, confirming your verbal request for annual leave from Monday 4 July to Friday 15 July. You are also required to state the remaining number of days you have left of your annual leave entitlement.

Use the items below to produce an appropriate email. You will not need to use all of the items.

From: **AATstudent@parrystores.com**	
To:	
Subject:	

Further to our conversation I wish to request annual leave from Monday 4 July to Friday 15 July. This will result in me having 4 further days of annual leave entitlement remaining.	Cheers AAT Student

I will be taking my holiday from 4 July to 15 July.	Hello Mary

Hello Mohan	4 July to 15 July	MNsingh@barrys.com	Kind regards AAT Student

Msingh@parrystores.com	Annual Leave Request

2.4 Organisations communicate using different styles and formats.

(a) **Show whether the following statements are True or False.**

Organisations use templates to save time as staff only have to input the key information.

True ☐

False ☐

Organisations use a 'house style' for documents because it ensures the image of the organisation is correctly portrayed.

True ☐

False ☐

You have received an electronic file containing data from the production department and have been asked to query some of the figures. This is a very urgent task as the figures have to be agreed by the end of today.

(b) **Select the most appropriate form of communication.**

Letter ☐

Report ☐

Email ☐

2.5 It is important to observe confidentiality.

(a) **Show whether the following statement is True or False.**

Confidential information can be left on your desk as long as you are not going to be away from your desk for longer than 1 hour.

True ☐

False ☐

(b) **Complete the following sentence by selecting the most appropriate option.**

You [   ] lock your computer when you leave your desk.

- should
- should not

2.6 Finance professionals and organisations have a duty to behave with integrity and act in a socially responsible manner.

Complete the statements by selecting the TWO appropriate items from the lists below. You will not need to use all of the items.

Statement	Item
A finance professional could renew job related technical knowledge by	

- attending an accountancy update course.
- attending a language course.
- reading the financial newspapers.
- reading the sports section of the newspaper.

Statement	Item
Examples of environmentally responsible policies are	

- using double sided printing to save paper.
- offering free tea and coffee to staff.
- offering flexi time working to staff.
- asking staff to use public transport wherever possible.

2.7 Organisations should observe health and safety guidelines.

(a) **Complete the following sentences by selecting the most appropriate item.**

An organisation is legally required to provide a [   ]

List items

warm
quiet
safe

environment [   ] .

List items

only for warehouse staff
only for office staff
for all staff and visitors

If an employee sees a hazard they [   ] required to report it.

List items

are not
are always
are sometimes

(b) **Show whether the following statement is True or False.**

Ensuring your desk is kept clean and tidy helps you to work more efficiently and promotes a better image to visitors.

True ☐

False ☐

2.8 It is important to understand the skills needed by a finance professional.

(a) **Complete the following sentences by selecting the most appropriate option.**

A finance professional should [   ]   have good design skills
                                                         have good numeracy skills

and show a [   ] attitude.   responsible
                                               fun loving

(b) **Complete the statement by selecting the TWO appropriate items from the lists below. You will not need to use all of the items.**

Statement	Item
A trainee finance professional should	———————————
	———————————

List items

- show a willingness to learn.
- not discuss their training needs with anyone.
- display a careless attitude.
- discuss their training needs with their manager.

2.9 It is important to work effectively.

It is Monday morning and you arrive at work to find there has been a water leak and all of the desks in the office except yours have been covered in water. Your colleagues are understandably upset.

(a)   **Which ONE of the following actions should you take?**

Ignore the situation and open your mail   ☐

Carry on with your work even though it is not urgent   ☐

Offer to help your colleagues   ☐

Planning is very important to help you meet your deadlines.

(b)   **Which ONE of the following documents below is a planning aid?**

A statement of profit or loss   ☐

A schedule of work   ☐

An invoice   ☐

It is important to use an appropriate form of communication at all times.

(c)   **Link the description to the appropriate form of communicating by drawing a line from the left hand box to the right hand box.**

A non electronic form of communication sent to a supplier requesting information about their new products.	**Email**
An electronic form of communication to be sent to the whole company advising them of the year end accounting procedures.	**Letter**
A non electronic form of communication sent to the sales department advising them of new reporting procedures.	**Memo**

2.10

- You work for Downs Electrics.

- You have been asked to write a letter to a supplier Clare Richmond at Capers, Maine Road, Newberry, BB6 2RP.

- You are to request a credit note for faulty goods received by Downs Electrics on 12 July 20XX and returned to Capers on 17 July 20XX.

- The faulty goods were 25 boxes of Product AB3 and were invoiced at £3,701.25 on invoice number 3629.

- Although it is unusual to receive faulty goods from Capers you are keen to get a credit note as the amount of £3,701.25 is shown as owing on the statement just received from Capers.

- Today's date is 26 July 20XX.

BPP
LEARNING MEDIA

Use the items below to produce an appropriate letter to Clare Richmond. You will not need to use all of the items.

Downs Electrics
Bradwell Road, Darsley, SS7 1BY

Dear Clare	Yours sincerely

Dear Sir	26 July 20XX

AAT Student
Accounts
Assistant

Yours faithfully

C Richmond
Capers
Maine Road
Newberry
BB6 2RP

The goods we received from you were no good.

Capsters
Oldberry

Return of Goods – request for credit note.

If you need to discuss the situation further do not hesitate to contact me.

Many thanks for your cooperation.

We want a credit note for these so we don't have to pay the amount on the statement.

On 12 July 20XX we received 25 boxes of Product AB3 as detailed on your invoice 3629. Unfortunately the quality of these products was not acceptable and we therefore returned them to you on 17 July 20XX.

We have just received a statement from you requesting payment of £3,701.25 for these goods and therefore ask that a credit note is raised as soon as possible for these items.

AAT sample assessment 2: answers

1.1

(a)

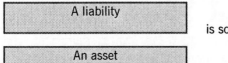

| A liability | is something an organisation owes. |
| An asset | is something an organisation owns. |

(b)

Item	Asset	Liability	Income	Expenditure
Sales			✓	
Electricity				✓

1.2

Description	Term
A transaction to sell goods when payment is made immediately	Cash sales
A transaction to purchase services when payment is made a month later.	Credit purchases

1.3

(a)

£ | 335.36

(b)

Some time after the oranges are sold.

1.4

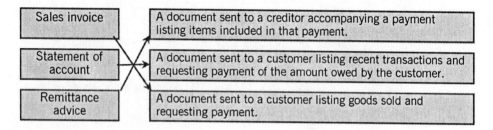

Sales invoice	A document sent to a creditor accompanying a payment listing items included in that payment.
Statement of account	A document sent to a customer listing recent transactions and requesting payment of the amount owed by the customer.
Remittance advice	A document sent to a customer listing goods sold and requesting payment.

1.5

(a)

An invoice sent to a customer

(b)

A cheque sent by a customer   ✓

(c)

Bateman Retail
19 White Lane, Conglefield, WA4 6TX
VAT Registration No. 176 39688 00
Invoice No. 2045

To: Gould Ltd   19 July 20XX
3 Granby Road,
Sailport SS1 2HS

	£
80 panels @ £4.35 each	348.00
VAT @ 20%	69.60
Total	417.60

Terms: 30 days net   **Book of prime entry**

| Purchases day-book |

Gould Ltd
3 Granby Road, Sailport, SS1 2HS
VAT Registration No. 397 3813 00
Credit note No. CN620

To: Mayfield
Associates   10 July 20XX
22 Lystral Lane,
Fleetbury FY5 2DT

	£
20 items of product AB2 @ £5.70 each	114.00
VAT @ 20%	22.80
Total	136.80

Book of prime entry | Sales returns day-book |

<table>
<tr><td colspan="2" align="center">**Gould Ltd**
Cash payments listing</td></tr>
<tr><td>20 July 20XX</td><td></td></tr>
<tr><td></td><td align="right">£</td></tr>
<tr><td>LH Hallsworth – for repairs to roof</td><td align="right">67.00</td></tr>
<tr><td>Express Cars – taxi fare</td><td align="right">35.60</td></tr>
<tr><td></td><td align="right">_____</td></tr>
<tr><td>Total</td><td align="right">102.60</td></tr>
<tr><td align="right">**Book of prime entry**</td><td>Cash payments book</td></tr>
</table>

1.6

Numerical

1.7

In a batch processing system a group of purchases invoices are entered into the accounting records at the same time.

True

1.8

(a)

Date:	County Bank plc Northport	£50 notes	150.00
24 July 20XX		£20 notes	
		£10 notes	50.00
	Account	£5 notes	
	Fraser Ltd	£2 coin	
		£1 coin	6.00
	Paid by	Other coin	1.10
		Total cash	207.10
	40-29-67 10672348	Cheques, POs	270.00
		Total £	477.10

(b) The person who should sign the 'Paid in by' section of the paying in slip should be the bank cashier.

False

1.9

(a)

11 July 20XX   ✓

(b)

Dawes Paints   ✓

(c)

One thousand three hundred and forty seven pounds and nine pence   ✓

(d)

The amount in words on a cheque should match exactly the amount in figures.

True   ✓

1.10

(a)

When income   **is more than**   expenditure this results in a profit.

(b)

(i)

£   146,000

(ii)

£   67,600

(c)

26   %

1.11

(a)

£   3.60

(b)

£   38

1.12

(a)

Region	Sales £
North	5,683.68
South	25,289.02
East	3,672.70
West	2,455.00
Total	37,100.40

(b)

£ 9,275.10

(c)

Store Code	Expenses £
N001	25,680.00
B010	34,210.90
S214	43,235.43
J967	6,420.00
Total	109,546.33

(d)

4:1

2.1

Organisation	Public sector	Private sector	Charitable sector
A shop selling goods specifically to raise funds for sick children			✓
The local police service	✓		

2.2

Information produced by the accounting department will only be used by managers in the accounting department.

False

Customers of the accounting department are always from outside of the organisation.

False

2.3

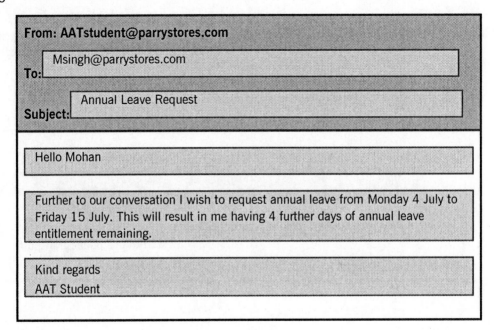

From: AATstudent@parrystores.com

To: Msingh@parrystores.com

Subject: Annual Leave Request

Hello Mohan

Further to our conversation I wish to request annual leave from Monday 4 July to Friday 15 July. This will result in me having 4 further days of annual leave entitlement remaining.

Kind regards
AAT Student

2.4

(a)

Organisations use templates to save time as staff only have to input the key information.

True

Organisations use a 'house style' for documents because it ensures the image of the organisation is correctly portrayed.

True

(b)

Email

2.5

(a)

Confidential information can be left on your desk as long as you are not going to be away from your desk for longer than 1 hour.

False ✓

(b)

You | should | lock your computer when you leave your desk.

2.6

Statement	Item
A finance professional could renew job related technical knowledge by	attending an accountancy update course.
	reading the financial newspapers.

Statement	Item
Examples of environmentally responsible policies are	using double sided printing to save paper.
	asking staff to use public transport wherever possible.

2.7

(a)

An organisation is legally required to provide a | safe | environment | for all staff and visitors. |

If an employee sees a hazard they | are always | required to report it.

(b)

Ensuring your desk is kept clean and tidy helps you to work more efficiently and promotes a better image to visitors.

True ✓

2.8

(a)

A finance professional should   **have good numeracy skills**   and show a

responsible   attitude.

(b)

Statement	Item
A trainee finance professional should	**show a willingness to learn.**
	discuss their training needs with their manager.

2.9

(a)

Offer to help your colleagues   ☑

(b)

A schedule of work.   ☑

(c)

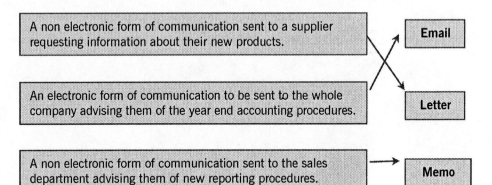

2.10

<table>
<tr><td colspan="2" align="center">**Downs Electrics**
Bradwell Road, Darsley, SS7 1BY</td></tr>
<tr><td colspan="2">26 July 20XX</td></tr>
<tr><td colspan="2">C Richmond
Capers
Maine Road
Newberry
BB6 2RP</td></tr>
<tr><td colspan="2">Dear Clare</td></tr>
<tr><td colspan="2">**Return of Goods – request for credit note**</td></tr>
<tr><td colspan="2">On 12 July 20XX we received 25 boxes of Product AB3 as detailed on your invoice 3629. Unfortunately the quality of these products was not acceptable and we therefore returned them to you on 17 July 20XX.</td></tr>
<tr><td colspan="2">We have just received a statement from you requesting payment of £3,701.25 for these goods and therefore ask that a credit note is raised as soon as possible for these items.</td></tr>
<tr><td colspan="2">If you need to discuss the situation further do not hesitate to contact me.
Many thanks for your cooperation.</td></tr>
<tr><td colspan="2">Yours sincerely</td></tr>
<tr><td colspan="2">AAT Student
Accounts Assistant</td></tr>
</table>

BPP practice assessment 1

1.1 Organisations have assets, liabilities, income and expenditure.

(a) **Which ONE of the following statements is FALSE?**

An asset is something an organisation owns. ☐

A liability is something an organisation owes. ☐

Income is something an organisation spends. ☐

(b) **Place a tick in the appropriate column of the table below to show whether each of the items listed is an example of an asset, a liability, income or expenditure. You should not place more than one tick (✓) against each item.**

Item	Asset	Liability	Income	Expenditure
Insurance				
Sale				
Bank loan				

1.2 It is important to understand the terminology used when buying and selling goods for cash and on credit.

Choose the appropriate term from the list below to match the description.

Description	Term described
A transaction to sell goods when payment is made at a later date than delivery of the goods.	
A transaction to buy goods when payment is made immediately.	

List of terms

Cash sale
Cash purchase
Credit sale
Credit purchase,
Debtor (receivable)
Creditor (payable)

BPP
LEARNING MEDIA

189

1.3 Your organisation purchased 12 boxes of paper for £60.72 in total from RG Office Supplies.

(a) **What is the cost of each box of paper?**

£ [   ]

RG Office Supplies agreed to issue an invoice asking your organisation to pay for the boxes of paper within 60 days.

(b) **Is the purchase of the boxes of paper a cash transaction or a credit transaction?**

[   ]

1.4 Organisations issue and receive different documents when buying and selling goods.

Complete the following sentences by selecting the most appropriate option from the list of terms below.

An organisation receives [   ] from a supplier

listing goods sold to the organisation and showing the amount due to be paid, and when it is due to be paid by.

An organisation receives [   ] from a supplier

showing the total amount the organisation owes in respect of credit sales, detailing the invoices that have not yet been paid.

An organisation sends [   ] to a supplier requesting

that the goods specified in the document be sold to the organisation.

List of terms

a purchase order
a receipt
a statement of account
an invoice

1.5 You work for Price Traders. You are preparing to record some documents in the books of prime entry.

(a) **Select which ONE of the documents below will be entered in the sales day book.**

A cheque sent by a customer [ ]

A credit note sent by a supplier [ ]

An invoice sent to a customer [✓]

(b) **Select which ONE of the documents below will be entered in the cash receipts book.**

An invoice sent by a supplier ☐

A cheque sent to a supplier ☐

A cheque sent by a customer ☑

(c) **Insert an item from the following list into the bottom right hand box on each document to show which book of prime entry that document will be entered into in Price Traders' books. You will not need to use all the items.**

- Cash payments book
- Cash receipts book
- Purchases day book
- Purchases returns day book
- Sales day book
- Sales returns day book

Price Traders

Unit 1, Industrial Park, Spantage, SP1 4LD.
VAT registration: 247 8597 00

Invoice number: 295300   4 March 20XX
To: Market Value Ltd

	£
58 items of product DTF @ £5.60 each	324.80
VAT @ 20%	64.96
TOTAL	389.76

Book of prime entry [   ]

Price Traders

Unit 1, Industrial Park, Spantage, SP1 4LD.
VAT registration: 247 8597 00

Credit note number: 3300   5 March 20XX
To: Auscon Ltd

	£
8 items of product CX @ £2.30 each	18.40
VAT @ 20%	3.68
TOTAL	22.08

Book of prime entry

Happy Wholesalers Ltd

12 High Street, Dillingford, DL3 5RP.
VAT registration: 207 9743 00

6 March 20XX   Credit note number: 89
To: Price Traders

	£
1 part ETD @ £20.00	20.00
VAT @ 20%	4.00
TOTAL	24.00

Book of prime entry

1.6 Some organisations use coding within the accounting records.

Show whether the following statement is True or False.

In an alphabetical coding system all codes consist of letters only.

True ☐

False ☐

1.7 Your organisation uses a batch processing system to enter sales invoices into the accounting records.

Show whether the following statement is True or False.

In the accounting system, sales invoices must be entered into the accounting records individually.

True ☐

False ☐

1.8 On 16 March 20XX you have been asked to pay the following items into Tricky Traders' bank account.

Six	£50 notes
Three	£20 notes
One	£5 note
Twenty	50 pence coins
Twelve	20 pence coins

(a) **Complete the paying-in slip below**

Date:	Date:	MIDWEST BANK	£50 notes	
A/C			£20 notes	
			£10 notes	
Cash:		Account name	£5 notes	
			£2 coins	
Cheques, POs			£1 coins	
		Paid in by	Other coin	
Total:			Total cash	
		29-09-99	Cheques, POs	
000894		9846968	Total £	

(b) **Show whether the following statement is True or False.**

Paying-in slips should not be dated by the person paying the money into the bank.

True ☐

False ☐

1.9 It is important to ensure cheques sent to suppliers are completed properly.

On 24 April 20XX you are preparing a cheque for three hundred and twenty-three pounds and fifty-five pence to send to a supplier, Woodcutter Ltd.

(a) **Which ONE of the following options shows the date as it should be written on the cheque?**

24 April 20XY

24.05.XX

24 April 20XX

(b) **Which ONE of the following options shows the payee as it should be written on the cheque?**

Woodcutters

Woodcutter Ltd

Woodcuter Ltd

(c) **Which ONE of the following options shows the amount in figures as it should be written on the cheque?**

£333.55

£323.55

£302.55

(d) **Show whether the following statement is True or False.**

The payee of a cheque is the person to whom payment is being made.

True   ☐

False   ☐

1.10 At the end of every year your organisation calculates the profit or loss for the year.

(a) **Show whether the following statement is True or False.**

Income less expenditure equals profit.

True   ☐

False   ☐

Last year your organisation recorded income and expenditure as shown in the table below.

Income and expenditure	£
Sales	1,000,000
Cost of sales	450,000
Payroll costs	250,000
Electricity	20,000
Distribution costs	10,000

(b) **Use the income and expenditure figures to complete the following calculations.**

   (i) **Calculate gross profit**

   £ [   ]

   (ii) **Calculate net profit**

   £ [   ]

(c) **Using your answer from (b)(ii), calculate net profit as a percentage of sales. If your answer is not a whole number make sure you give your answer to two decimal places.**

   [   ] %

1.11 An organisation is reviewing the selling price of some of its products.

The current selling price of product number 598 is £36.80. This is to be increased by $\frac{1}{8}$ (one eighth).

(a) **Calculate the increase in selling price for product number 598.**

   £ [   ]

The current selling price of product number 396 is £21.00. This is to be increased by 7%.

(b) **Calculate the increase in selling price for product number 396.**

   £ [   ]

1.12 Your organisation keeps detailed records of costs.

Service and repair costs for each of four delivery vehicles are shown in the table below.

(a) **Complete the table to show the service and repair costs for Vehicle 2.**

Delivery vehicles	£
Vehicle 1	375.66
Vehicle 2	
Vehicle 3	496.55
Vehicle 4	1,035.12
Total	2,408.60

(b) **Calculate the average service and repair cost per vehicle.**

£

Costs relating to advertising and marketing are shown in the table below.

(c) **Complete the table to show the total advertising and marketing costs.**

Item	£
Marketing	200.60
Advertising	2,104.60
Consultant	526.15
Sundries	137.45
Total	

(d) **Which of the following is the ratio of the cost of advertising to the cost of the consultant?**

- 3:1
- 4:1
- 5:1

2.1   There are different types of organisation.

Complete the following sentences by selecting the most appropriate option from the list of items below each sentence.

(a)   The Fire Service is a ⬚ organisation.

- ▪ private sector
- ▪ public sector
- ▪ charitable

(b)   A limited company in the private sector ⬚

aim to make a profit.

- ▪ does
- ▪ does not

2.2   It is important to understand the role of the accounting department within an organisation.

Show whether the following statements are True or False.

(a)   Information provided by the accounting department is used by managers within the organisation to make poorer business decisions.

True   ☐

False   ☐

(b)   An example of a customer of the accounting department is the sales department of the company.

True   ☐

False   ☐

2.3   You work for ABC Chemicals and have been asked to send an email to Andy Poole, your manager, confirming your attendance at the annual staff conference on 1 and 2 June and requesting overnight accommodation on 1 June.

Using the items below, compose an appropriate email in the template given.

You will not need to use all of the items.

From:	AATstudent@abcchemicals.com
To:	
Subject:	

andypoole@abcchemicals.com

Confirmation

Annual Staff Conference: Confirmation of attendance

Hi Andy

Please accept this email as confirmation of my attendance at the staff conference on 1 and 2 June. As it is over two days I request overnight accommodation on 1 June.

Kind regards
AAT student

andypoole@abchemicals.com

Hello Andy

I am confirming I want to attend in June and need to stay overnight.

Cheers
AAT student

2.4 Organisations communicate using different styles and formats.

(a) **Show whether the following statements are True or False.**

Organisations use templates to present a positive, consistent view of their organisation.

True   ☐

False   ☐

Organisations use a 'house style' for documents because it helps customers know documents are genuine.

True   ☐

False   ☐

You have been asked to send a credit note to a potential customer.

(b) **Select the most appropriate form of communication to accompany the credit note.**

☐   Letter

☐   Memo

☐   Report

2.5 It is important to observe confidentiality.

Complete the following sentences by inserting the most appropriate option from the list below each sentence.

Information about staff bonuses held on the computer should be kept

| |
| |

- in an area to which all employees have access.
- in a password protected file with access restricted to those who need the information.

A friend is a supplier of the organisation where you work. She asks you how much profit your organisation is making on items sold on. You reply:

| |
| |

- 'I am sorry but I cannot give you any information as it is confidential.'
- 'As you are a supplier I can tell you that we add 25%.'

2.6 Finance professionals and organisations have a duty to behave in a professional and environmentally responsible manner.

Complete each sentence in the following table by inserting the most appropriate item from the list below. You will not need to use all of the items.

Sentence	Item
Once accountants are qualified...	
An accountant should always...	
An organisation should adopt socially responsible practices because...	
An example of an environmentally responsible policy is to ...	

- ... put personal needs above the requirements of the organisation.
- ... they should complete sufficient training to maintain professional competence.
- ... behave with honesty and integrity.
- ... it has a duty to act ethically.
- ... lobby governments on environmental issues.
- ... use recycled paper.

2.7 Organisations should observe health and safety guidelines.

(a) **Complete this sentence by inserting the most appropriate option from the list below each box.**

An organisation ⬚ to provide a safe environment for ⬚

has a duty   staff only.
has a choice whether   visitors only.
does not have   anyone.

(b) **Show whether the following statements are True or False.**

An employee has a duty to report unsafe practice to a manager.

True ☐

False ☐

It is important to keep a tidy desk for health and safety reasons.

True ☐

False ☐

2.8 It is important to understand the skills and attributes needed by a finance professional.

(a) **Complete this sentence by inserting the most appropriate option from the list below each box.**

A finance professional should ▢   be numerate
   be creative

and be able to show ▢   a professional attitude.
   an unprofessional attitude.

(b) **Show whether the following statements are True or False.**

A finance professional can acquire knowledge by shadowing a more senior member of staff.

True   ▢

False   ▢

Somebody who is training to be a finance professional should meet regularly with their manager to discuss their specific training needs.

True   ▢

False   ▢

2.9 It is important to work effectively.

(a) **Answer the following questions by selecting the most appropriate option.**

It is Monday, it is nearly the end of the day and you have completed all of your tasks for the day. Your colleague has just received a report which she must process this evening. If the report is not processed today the whole department will be behind for the rest of the week. She will only be able to complete the report today by rushing the work and not doing a thorough job.

Which ONE of the following actions should you take?

▢   Tidy your desk to make sure it is clear for next week.

▢   Go to your colleague and ask her if there is anything you could do to help her.

▢   Go home.

Planning is very important to help you meet your deadlines.

Which ONE of the following documents below is a planning aid?

☐   Credit note

☐   Diary

☐   Holiday request form

It is important to use an appropriate form of communication at all times.

(b)   **Link the description to the appropriate form of communication by drawing a line from each left hand box to the appropriate right hand box.**

An electronic form of communication which may be sent both within and outside of the organisation.	Report
A formal written form of communication sent from one employee to another within and outside of the organisation.	Email
An informal written form of communication usually sent from one employee to another within the organisation.	Memo

2.10 You work for Smith and Co. You have been asked to send a copy of the draft management accounts to all the directors. You have been asked to send a memo with the accounts, confirming that the directors should read the accounts and have prepared their comments about them for the meeting on Friday 5 April 20XX. The date today is 24 March 20XX.

Using the items below, compose an appropriate memo in the box below. You will not need to use all of the items.

| 24 March 20XX | Directors | Cheers | Everybody |

| 5 April 20XX | Dear Sirs | Thank you | Directors |

| Management accounts | Meeting 5 April 20XX | AAT student Accounts Assistant |

| Please find the draft management accounts enclosed with this memo. | AAT student Accounts Assistant |

| Please ensure that you have read the accounts, and prepared your comments, in time for the meeting on 5 April 20XX. |

| Please ensure that you have read the accounts, and prepared your comments, in time for the meeting on 24 March 20XX. |

| Read them and have something to say in the meeting (5 April 20XX). |

| Yours faithfully | Yours sincerely |

MEMO

To: _____

From: _____

Date: _____

Subject: _____

BPP practice assessment 1: answers

1.1 (a) Income is something an organisation spends.

(b)

Item	Asset	Liability	Income	Expenditure
Insurance				✓
Sale			✓	
Bank loan		✓		

1.2

Description	Term described
A transaction to sell goods when payment is made at a later date than delivery of the goods.	Credit sale
A transaction to buy goods when payment is made immediately.	Cash purchase

1.3 (a) £   5.06

(b)   **Credit transaction**

1.4 An organisation receives **an invoice** from a supplier listing goods sold to the organisation and showing the amount due to be paid, and when it is due to be paid by.

An organisation receives **a statement of account** from a supplier showing the total amount the organisation owes in respect of credit sales, detailing the invoices that have not yet been paid.

An organisation sends **a purchase order** to a supplier requesting that the goods specified in the document be sold to the organisation.

1.5 (a) An invoice sent to a customer ☑

(b) A cheque sent by a customer ☑

(c)

Price Traders

Unit 1, Industrial Park, Spantage, SP1 4LD.
VAT registration: 247 8597 00

Invoice number: 295300   4 March 20XX
To: Market Value Ltd

	£
58 items of product DTF @ £5.60 each	324.80
VAT @ 20%	64.96
TOTAL	389.76

Book of prime entry   **Sales day book**

Price Traders

Unit 1, Industrial Park, Spantage, SP1 4LD.
VAT registration: 247 8597 00

Credit note number: 3300   5 March 20XX
To: Auscon Ltd

	£
8 items of product CX @ £2.30 each	18.40
VAT @ 20%	3.68
TOTAL	22.08

Book of prime entry   **Sales returns day book**

Happy Wholesalers Ltd

12 High Street, Dillingford, DL3 5RP.
VAT registration: 207 9743 00

6 March 20XX   Credit note number: 89
To: Price Traders

	£
1 part ETD @ £20.00	20.00
VAT @ 20%	4.00
TOTAL	24.00

Book of prime entry   **Purchases returns day book**

1.6 In an alphabetical coding system all codes consist of letters only.

True

1.7 In the accounting system, sales invoices must be entered into the accounting records individually.

False

1.8 (a)

Date: **16.3.XX**	Date:	MIDWEST BANK	£50 notes	**£300.00**
A/C **9846968**	**16 March 20XX**		£20 notes	**£60.00**
			£10 notes	
Cash: **£377.40**		Account name	£5 notes	**£5.00**
		Tricky Traders	£2 coins	
Cheques, POs			£1 coins	
		Paid in by	Other coin	**£12.40**
Total: **£377.40**		**A Student**	Total cash	**£377.40**
		29-09-99	Cheques, POs	
000894		9846968	Total £	**£377.40**

(b) Paying-in slips should not be dated by the person paying the money into the bank.

False

1.9 (a) 24 April 20XX

(b) Woodcutter Ltd

(c) £323.55

(d) The payee of a cheque is the person to whom payment is being made.

True   ☑

1.10 (a) Income less expenditure equals profit.

True   ☑

(b) (i) £ 550,000

(ii) £ 270,000

(c) 27 %

1.11 (a) The increase in selling price for product number 598

£ 4.60

(b) The increase in selling price for product number 396

£ 1.47

1.12 (a) Service and repair costs for Vehicle 2

Delivery vehicles	£
Vehicle 1	375.66
Vehicle 2	501.27
Vehicle 3	496.55
Vehicle 4	1,035.12
Total	2,408.60

(b) The average service and repair cost per vehicle

£   602.15

(c) Total advertising and marketing costs

Item	£
Marketing	200.60
Advertising	2,104.60
Consultant	526.15
Sundries	137.45
Total	**2,968.80**

(d) The ratio of the cost of advertising to the cost of the consultant

4 : 1

2.1 (a) The Fire Service is a  **public sector** organisation.

(b) A limited company in the private sector **does**

aim to make a profit.

2.2 (a) Information provided by the accounting department is used by managers within the organisation to make poorer business decisions.

False

(b) An example of a customer of the accounting department is the sales department of the company.

True

2.3

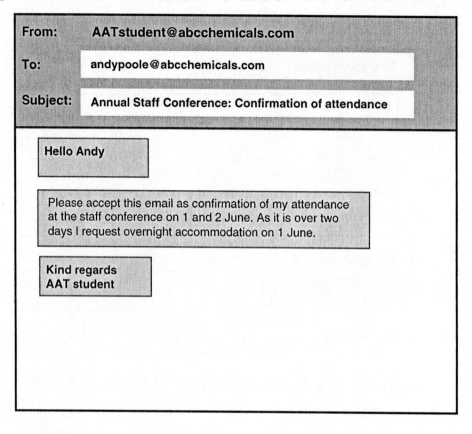

From:	AATstudent@abcchemicals.com
To:	andypoole@abcchemicals.com
Subject:	Annual Staff Conference: Confirmation of attendance

Hello Andy

Please accept this email as confirmation of my attendance at the staff conference on 1 and 2 June. As it is over two days I request overnight accommodation on 1 June.

Kind regards
AAT student

2.4 (a) Organisations use templates to present a positive, consistent view of their organisation.

True ✓

Organisations use a 'house style' for documents because it helps customers know documents are genuine.

True ✓

(b) The most appropriate form of communication to accompany the credit note

✓ Letter

2.5 Information about staff bonuses held on the computer should be kept **in a password protected file with access restricted to those who need the information.**

A friend is a supplier of the organisation where you work. She asks you how much profit your organisation is making on items sold on. You reply: **'I am sorry but I cannot give you any information as it is confidential'.**

2.6

Sentence	Item
Once accountants are qualified...	**... they should complete sufficient training to maintain professional competence.**
An accountant should always...	**... behave with honesty and integrity.**
An organisation should adopt socially responsible practices because...	**... it has a duty to act ethically.**
An example of an environmentally responsible policy is to ...	**... use recycled paper.**

2.7 Organisations should observe health and safety guidelines.

(a) An organisation **has a duty** to provide a safe environment for **anyone.**

(b) An employee has a duty to report unsafe practice to a manager.

True   ☑

It is important to keep a tidy desk for health and safety reasons.

True   ☑

2.8 It is important to understand the skills and attributes needed by a finance professional.

(a) A finance professional should **be numerate** and be able to show

a professional attitude.

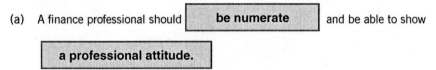

(b)   A finance professional can acquire knowledge by shadowing a more senior member of staff.

True

Somebody who is training to be a finance professional meets regularly with their manager to discuss their specific training needs.

True

2.9 (a)   The most appropriate option is:

☑   Go to your colleague and ask her if there is anything you could do to help her.

The following document is a planning aid.

☑   Diary.

(b)

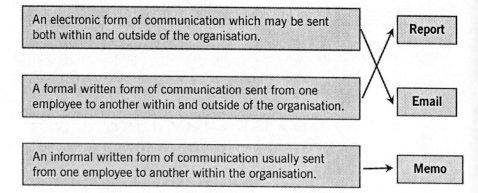

An electronic form of communication which may be sent both within and outside of the organisation.	Report
A formal written form of communication sent from one employee to another within and outside of the organisation.	Email
An informal written form of communication usually sent from one employee to another within the organisation.	Memo

2.10

MEMO		
To:	**Directors**	
From:	**AAT student, Accounts Assistant**	
Date:	**24 March 20XX**	
Subject:	**Management accounts**	

Please find the draft management accounts enclosed with this memo.

Please ensure that you have read the accounts, and prepared your comments, in time for the meeting on 5 April 20XX.

Thank you

AAT student
Accounts Assistant

BPP practice assessment 2

1.1 Organisations have assets, liabilities, income and expenditure.

   (a) **Which ONE of the following statements is true?**

      Expenditure is something an organisation owes. ☐

      A liability is something an organisation owns. ☐

      Income is something an organisation earns. ☐

   (b) **Place a tick in the appropriate column of the table below to show whether each of the items listed is an example of an asset, a liability, income or expenditure. You should not place more than one tick (✓) against each item.**

Item	Asset	Liability	Income	Expenditure
Bank interest received				
Overdraft fee				
Inventory				

1.2 It is important to understand the terminology used when buying and selling goods for cash and on credit.

Choose the appropriate term from the list below to match the description.

Description	Term described
The amount that will be paid by the organisation at a later date in respect of a credit purchase.	
The amount that will be paid to the organisation at a later date in respect of a credit sale.	

List of terms

Cash sale
Cash purchase
Credit sale
Credit purchase
Debtor (receivable)
Creditor (payable)

1.3 Your organisation sold 8 desks for £240.40 in total to JP Fitters Company.

(a) **What is the price of each desk?**

£ [   ]

Your organisation issued an invoice asking JP Fitters Company to pay for the desks within 30 days.

(b) **Is the sale of the desks a cash transaction or a credit transaction?**

[   ]

1.4 Organisations issue and receive different documents when buying and selling goods.

Complete the following sentences by selecting the most appropriate option from the list below.

An organisation sends [   ] to a customer listing

goods sold to the customer and showing the amount due to be paid, and when it is due to be paid.

An organisation gives [   ] to a customer for goods

bought with cash.

An organisation receives [   ] from a customer

requesting that the goods specified in the document be sold to the customer.

List of terms

a purchase order
a receipt
a statement of account
an invoice

1.5 You work for Smyth Traders. You are preparing to record some documents in the books of prime entry.

(a) **Select which ONE of the documents below will be entered in the purchases returns day book.**

A credit note sent by a supplier   [ ]

A cheque sent to a supplier   [ ]

A credit note sent to a customer   [ ]

(b) **Select which ONE of the documents below will be entered in the purchases day book.**

A cheque sent to a supplier ☐

An invoice sent by a supplier ☐

A credit note sent by a supplier ☐

(c) **Fill in the boxes on each document given below to show which book of prime entry that document will be entered into. Select your answer from one of the following options.**

Options

Cash payments book
Cash receipts book
Purchases day book
Purchases returns day book
Sales day book
Sales returns day book

MIDWEST BANK
Midwest Bank Business Centre, High Street   34-04-32
                                                      40599682
                                        Date 24 March 20XX

Pay Whittaker Traders Ltd only

Three hundred and twenty pounds and twenty five pence | £320.25 |

                                          for Smyth Traders

300593   340432   40599682

Book of prime entry   [   ]

Date:	MIDWEST BANK	£50 notes	
23 March 20XX	Tuddenham	£20 notes	
		£10 notes	
	Account	£5 notes	
	Smyth Traders	£2 coins	
		£1 coins	
	Paid in by	Other coin	
	Marion Green	Total cash	
	34-04-32	Cheques, POs	£3,592
	40599682	Total £	£3,592

Book of prime entry

Khan Enterprises

Unit 7, Westford Industrial Park, WF23 6TD

VAT Registration No: 529 5999 00

INVOICE NUMBER: P3953945

INVOICE DATE: 14 March 20XX

To: Smyth Traders, 6 Church Street, Tuddenham

	£
24 items of product DG @ £100.99 each	2,423.76
VAT @ 20%	484.75
Total	2,908.51

Book of prime entry

1.6 Some organisations use coding within the accounting records.

Show whether the following statement is True or False.

In a alphanumerical coding system codes consist of a combination of letters and numbers.

True ☐

False ☐

1.7 Your organisation uses a batch processing system.

Show whether the following statement is True or False.

Purchase invoices may be batched, and entered into the accounting system together.

True ☐

False ☐

1.8 On 6 March 20XX you have been asked to pay the following items into Taylor Trading Ltd's bank account.

Four	£20 notes
Twelve	£10 notes
Four	£5 notes
Two	£2 coins
Six	£1 coins
A cheque	£574.88

(a) **Complete the paying-in slip below**

Date:	Date:	GLOBAL BANK	£50 notes	
A/C 46898468			£20 notes	
			£10 notes	
Cash:		Account name	£5 notes	
			£2 coins	
Cheques, POs			£1 coins	
		Paid in by	Other coin	
Total:			Total cash	
		34-16-59	Cheques, POs	
010395		46898468	Total £	

(b) **Show whether the following statement is True or False.**

A person paying money into a bank should sign the paying-in slip.

True ☐

False ☐

1.9 It is important to ensure cheques sent to suppliers are completed properly.

On 14 April 20XY you are preparing a cheque for five hundred and forty-five pounds and two pence to send to a supplier, Easy Easels.

(a) **Which ONE of the following options shows the date as it should be written on the cheque?**

14.5.XY

14 April 20XY

14 April XY

(b) **Which ONE of the following options shows the payee as it should be written on the cheque?**

Easys

Easels

Easy Easels

(c) **Which ONE of the following options shows the amount in figures as it should be written on the cheque?**

£545.02

£545.20

£500.45

(d) **Show whether the following statement is True or False.**

The date on the cheque should be the day it is likely to arrive at the supplier's premises.

True ☐

False ☐

1.10 At the end of every year your organisation calculates the profit or loss for the year.

(a) **Show whether the following statement is True or False.**

If income exceeds expenditure, the organisation has made a loss.

True ☐

False ☐

Last year your organisation recorded income and expenditure as shown in the table below.

Income and expenditure	£
Sales	890,000
Cost of sales	653,780
Labour	124,740
Administration	45,700
Motor costs	800

(b)   **Use the income and expenditure figures to complete the following calculations.**

    (i)   **Calculate gross profit**

       £ [   ]

    (ii)   **Calculate net profit**

       £ [   ]

(c)   **Using your answer from (b)(ii), calculate net profit as a percentage of sales. If your answer is not a whole number make sure you give your answer up to two decimal places.**

    [   ] %

1.11 An organisation is reviewing the selling price of some of its products.

The current selling price of product number 59 is £16.60. This is to be increased by $\frac{1}{4}$ (one quarter).

(a)   **Calculate the increase in selling price for product number 59.**

    £ [   ]

The current selling price of product number 36 is £8.50. This is to be increased by 2%.

(b)   **Calculate the increase in selling price for product number 36.**

    £ [   ]

1.12 Your organisation keeps detailed records of costs.

Repair costs for each of four production machines are shown in the table below.

(a)   **Complete the table to show the Repair costs for Machine 1.**

	£
Machine 1	[ ]
Machine 2	208.12
Machine 3	345.77
Machine 4	105.11
Total	816.20

(b) **Calculate the average service and repair cost per machine.**

£ [   ]

Key costs relating to Factory 1 are shown in the table below.

(c) **Complete the table to show the total key costs relating to Factory 1.**

Item	£
Electricity	1,200.50
Wages	3,450.20
Security	51.15
Insurance	153.45
Total key costs	[ ]

(d) **Which of the following is the ratio of the cost of insurance to the cost of security?**

Options

3:1
4:1
5:1

[   ]

2.1 There are different types of organisation.

Complete the following sentences by selecting the most appropriate option from the list of items below each sentence.

(a) A partnership is a [   ] organisation.

- private sector
- public sector
- charitable

(b) A sole trader [   ] aim to make a profit.

- does
- does not

2.2 It is important to understand the role of the accounting department within an organisation.

Show whether the following statements are True or False.

(a) Information provided by the accounting department to other departments should be complete, accurate and timely.

True ☐

False ☐

(b) An example of a customer of the accounting department is the general public.

True ☐

False ☐

2.3 You work for MK Manufacturing and have been asked to send an email to Chris Cairns, the production manager, confirming the number of parts of XY that have been purchased in the year to date.

Using the items on the next page, compose an appropriate email in the template below.

You will not need to use all of the items.

From: AATstudent@MKM.com
To:
Subject:

chriscairns@MKM.com	XY parts

Purchases of XY parts year to date	Hi Chris

Please could you confirm the total number of XY parts that have been purchased in the year to date.	Kind regards AAT student

chrischairns@MKM.com	Hello Chris

How many XY parts have you bought this year?	Cheers AAT student

2.4 Organisations communicate using different styles and formats.

(a) **Show whether the following statements are True or False.**

Organisations use templates to save time in preparing documents.

True ☐

False ☐

Organisations use a 'house style' for documents because they are required to by law.

True ☐

False ☐

You have been asked to send an application pack to someone enquiring after a job in your organisation.

(b) **Select the most appropriate form of communication to accompany the application pack.**

☐ Letter

☐ Memo

☐ Report

2.5 It is important to observe confidentiality.

Complete the following sentences by inserting the most appropriate option from the list below each sentence.

Gail is working on the payroll. She leaves her desk to make a cup of tea. She should:

- Leave the payroll documents on her desk, as she'll only be gone five minutes.
- Lock the payroll documents in her desk drawer because she will be away from her desk.

A friend is a journalist, writing a story on local businesses for the local paper. She asks you how many people your organisation employs. You reply:

- '200'.
- 'I don't think it is appropriate for you to ask me, you should request a meeting with the managing director'.

2.6 Finance professionals and organisations have a duty to behave in a professional and environmentally responsible manner.

Complete each sentence in the following table by inserting the most appropriate item from the list below. You will not need to use all the items.

Sentence	Item
A qualified accountant should...	
Integrity is...	
An organisation should adopt socially responsible practices because...	
It is not environmentally responsible for a company when staff ...	

- ... keep up to date with technical requirements.
- ... not a key requirement for an accountant.
- ... an important characteristic for accountants.
- ... the general public wants it to.
- ... it impacts on the environment through its operations.
- ... print out copies of emails that could be stored online.

BPP
LEARNING MEDIA

2.7 Organisations should observe health and safety guidelines.

(a) **Complete this sentence by inserting the most appropriate option from the list below each box.**

An employee [   ] to behave in a [   ]

has a duty	safe manner.
has a choice whether	risk free manner.
does not have	respectful manner.

(b) **Show whether the following statements are True or False.**

Power cables to Tracy's computer trail across a corridor next to her desk. This is appropriate.

True   [ ]

False   [ ]

JP Trailers is a no smoking zone. Peter sees Zain smoking in the stationery cupboard. Peter should report Zain to a superior.

True   [ ]

False   [ ]

2.8 It is important to understand the skills and attributes needed by a finance professional.

(a) **Complete this sentence by inserting the most appropriate option from the list next to each box.**

A finance professional should [   ]   be punctual
                                                 be practical

and be able to show a [   ]   willingness to learn.
                                         willingness to teach.

(b) **Show whether the following statements are True or False.**

Reading a journal is an example of undertaking formal training.

True   [ ]

False   [ ]

Someone who is training to be a finance professional should discuss the training they have done with a supervisor to ensure that the new skills can be used in the organisation.

True ☐

False ☐

2.9 It is important to work effectively.

(a) **Answer the following questions by selecting the most appropriate option.**

You are working on a project that has to be finished by the end of the week. You have been given permission to attend a medical appointment on Friday morning, but it is looking like you will not have time to finish your section of the project in the time remaining on Friday. If the project runs over to Monday morning, the whole team will be inconvenienced.

Which ONE of the following actions should you NOT take?

☐   Tell your supervisor that you might not meet the deadline so that staff can be allocated to help you.

☐   Keep a record of the work you have done on the project, and the outstanding work so that other team members will be able to follow what you have done.

☐   Cancel your medical appointment.

Planning is very important to help you meet your deadlines.

Which ONE of the following documents below is a planning aid?

☐   Schedule

☐   Statement of account

☐   Stationery

It is important to use an appropriate form of communication at all times.

(b)   **Link the description to the appropriate form of communication by drawing a line from each left hand box to the appropriate right hand box.**

A written form of communication usually sent from a person in one organisation to a person in another organisation.	Report

A formal written form of communication sent both within and outside of the organisation.	Memo

An informal written form of communication usually sent from one employee to another within the organisation.	Letter

2.10 ■ You work for Weston Traders.

■ You have been asked to write a letter to a potential supplier, Miss A Singh, at AA Advertising, High Road, Colston, KC7 1WK.

■ You are to confirm the appointment with her which is due to take place in a week's time, on 5 May 20XX, at 2pm.

■ At the appointment she will be giving a presentation on behalf of her company to try to win a contract for a large advertising campaign Weston Traders wants to undertake.

■ Weston Traders' staff attending will be Mark Sprout, Managing Director, and Andy Singer, Financial Controller.

Using the items below, compose an appropriate letter in the box below. You will not need to use all of the items.

5 May 20XX	Dear Miss Singh	Dear Madam	Yours faithfully

Confirmation of appointment: 5 May 20XX at 2pm	Yours sincerely	28 April 20XX

I am writing on behalf of the Financial Controller to confirm the above appointment at which you are to give a presentation on behalf of your firm, AA Advertising.

I am writing on behalf of the Financial Controller to confirm the above appointment at which you are to give a presentation on behalf of your firm, ABC Advertising.

Weston Traders' staff attending the presentation will be Marc Sprout, Managing Controller, and Andy Singer, Financial Director

Weston Traders' staff attending the presentation will be Mark Sprout, Managing Director, and Andy Singer, Financial Controller.

They look forward to meeting you and learning more about what your company could do for our organisation.	A Singh AA Advertising High Road Colston KC7 1WK	A Singh ABC Advertising High Road Colston KC7 1WK

They look forward to meeting you and learning more about what your company could do for our organisation.	AAT student Accounts Assistant	Advertising presentation

Weston Traders
Castle St, Weston, KC6 7SC

BPP practice assessment 2: answers

1.1 (a) Income is something an organisation earns. ☑

(b)

Item	Asset	Liability	Income	Expenditure
Bank interest received			✓	
Overdraft fee				✓
Inventory	✓			

1.2

Description	Term described
The amount that will be paid by the organisation at a later date in respect of a credit purchase.	Creditor (Payable)
The amount that will be paid to the organisation at a later date in respect of a credit sale.	Debtor (Receivable)

1.3 (a) £ | 30.05 |

(b) | **Credit transaction** |

1.4 An organisation sends **an invoice** to a customer listing goods sold to the customer and showing the amount due to be paid, and when it is due to be paid.

An organisation gives **a receipt** to a customer for goods bought with cash.

An organisation receives **a purchase order** from a customer requesting that the goods specified in the document be sold to the customer.

1.5 (a) A credit note sent by a supplier ☑

(b) An invoice sent by a supplier ☑

(c)

MIDWEST BANK

Midwest Bank Business Centre, High Street   34-04-32

40599682

Date 24 March 20XX

Pay Whittaker Traders Ltd only

Three hundred and twenty pounds and twenty five pence   £320.25

for Smyth Traders

300593   340432   40599682   ∧⅃ᔕᕁ

Book of prime entry	Cash payments book

Date:	MIDWEST BANK	£50 notes	
23 March 20XX	Tuddenham	£20 notes	
		£10 notes	
	Account	£5 notes	
	Smyth Traders	£2 coins	
		£1 coins	
	Paid in by	Other coin	
	Marion Green	Total cash	
	34-04-32	Cheques, POs	£3,592
	40599682	Total £	£3,592

Book of prime entry	Cash receipts book

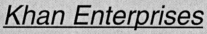

Khan Enterprises

Unit 7, Westford Industrial Park, WF23 6TD
VAT Registration No: 529 5999 00

INVOICE NUMBER: P3953945
INVOICE DATE: 14 March 20XX

To: Smyth Traders, 6 Church Street, Tuddenham

	£
24 items of product DG @ £100.99 each	2,423.76
VAT @ 20%	484.75
Total	2,908.51

Book of prime entry	**Purchases day book**

1.6 In a alphanumerical coding system all codes consist of a combination of letters and numbers.

True

1.7 Purchase invoices may be batched, and entered into the accounting system together.

True

1.8 (a)

Date: **6.3.XX**	Date:	GLOBAL BANK	£50 notes	
A/C 46898468	**6 March 20XX**		£20 notes	**£80**
			£10 notes	**£120**
Cash: **£230**		Account name	£5 notes	**£20**
		Taylor Trading Ltd	£2 coins	**£4**
Cheques, Pos			£1 coins	**£6**
£574.88		Paid in by	Other coin	
Total: **£804.88**		**A student**	Total cash	**£230**
		34-16-59	Cheques, POs	**£574.88**
		46898468		
010395			Total £	**£804.88**

(b) A person paying money into a bank should sign the paying-in slip.

True

1.9 (a) 14 April 20XY

(b) Easy Easels

(c) £545.02

(d) The date on the cheque should be the day it is likely to arrive at the supplier's premises.

False

1.10 At the end of every year your organisation calculates the profit or loss for the year.

(a) If income exceeds expenditure, the organisation has made a loss.

False

(b) (i) £ 236,220

(ii) £ 64,980

(c) 7.30 %

1.11 (a) The increase in selling price for product number 59

£   4.15

(b) The increase in selling price for product number 36

£   0.17

1.12 (a) Repair costs for Machine 1

	£
Machine 1	157.20
Machine 2	208.12
Machine 3	345.77
Machine 4	105.11
Total	816.20

(b) The average service and repair cost per machine

£   204.05

(c) Total key costs relating to Factory 1

Item	£
Electricity	1,200.50
Wages	3,450.20
Security	51.15
Insurance	153.45
Total key costs	4,855.30

(d) The ratio of the cost of insurance to the cost of security

3 : 1

2.1 (a) A partnership is a   **private sector**   organisation.

(b) A sole trader   **does**   aim to make a profit.

2.2 (a) Information provided by the accounting department to other departments should be complete, accurate and timely.

True ☑

(b) An example of a customer of the accounting department is the general public.

False ☑

2.3

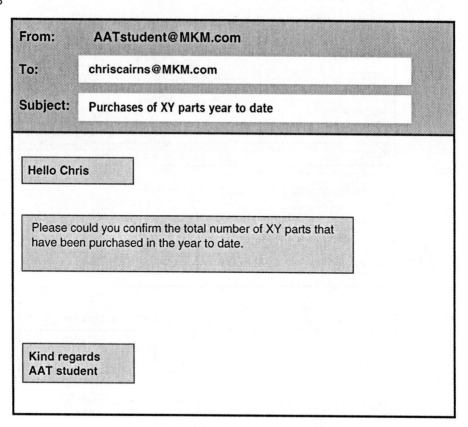

From:	AATstudent@MKM.com
To:	chriscairns@MKM.com
Subject:	Purchases of XY parts year to date

Hello Chris

Please could you confirm the total number of XY parts that have been purchased in the year to date.

Kind regards
AAT student

2.4 (a) Organisations use templates to save time in preparing documents.

True ☑

Organisations use a 'house style' for documents because they are required to by law.

False ☑

(b) The most appropriate form of communication to accompany the application pack.

☑ Letter

2.5 Gail is working on the payroll. She leaves her desk to make a cup of tea. She should:

Lock the payroll documents in her desk drawer because she will be away from her desk.

A friend is a journalist, writing a story on local businesses for the local paper. She asks you how many people your organisation employs. You reply:

'I don't think it is appropriate for you to ask me, you should request a meeting with the managing director'.

2.6

Sentence	Item
A qualified accountant should...	**... keep up to date with technical requirements.**
Integrity is...	**... an important characteristic for accountants.**
An organisation should adopt socially responsible practices because...	**... it impacts on the environment through its operations.**
It is not environmentally responsible for a company when staff ...	**... print out copies of emails that could be stored online.**

2.7 Organisations should observe health and safety guidelines.

(a) An employee  **has a duty** to behave in a **safe manner.**

(b) Power cables to Tracy's computer trail across a corridor next to her desk. This is appropriate.

False ☑

JP Trailers is a no smoking zone. Peter sees Zain smoking in the stationery cupboard. Peter should report Zain to a superior.

True ☑

2.8 It is important to understand the skills and attributes needed by a finance professional.

(a) A finance professional should | **be punctual** |

and be able to show a | **willingness to learn.** |

(b) Reading a journal is an example of undertaking formal training.

False ✓

Somebody who is training to be a finance professional should discuss the training they have done with a supervisor to ensure that the new skills can be used in the organisation.

True ✓

2.9 (a) The most appropriate option is:

✓ Cancel your medical appointment.

This question makes clear that you are working as part of a team so the other two options are reasonable responses to the tight deadline. It is not in your company's interest for you not to attend a medical appointment (you are not told in the question whether it is a significant appointment or not).

The following document is a planning aid

✓ Schedule

(b)

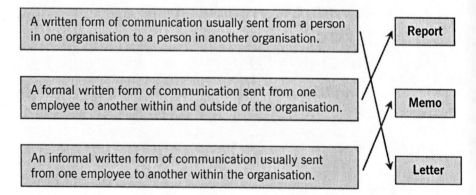

2.10

Weston Traders
Castle St, Weston, KC6 7SC

A Singh
AA Advertising
High Road
Colston
KC7 1WK

28 April 20XX

Dear Miss Singh

Confirmation of appointment: 5 May 20XX at 2pm

I am writing on behalf of the Financial Controller to confirm the above appointment at which you are to give a presentation on behalf of your firm, AA Advertising.

Weston Traders' staff attending the presentation will be Mark Sprout, Managing Director, and Andy Singer, Financial Controller.

They look forward to meeting you and learning more about what your company could do for our organisation.

Yours sincerely

AAT student
Accounts Assistant

Index

REVIEW FORM

How have you used this Workbook?
(Tick one box only)

☐ Home study

☐ On a course_____

☐ Other _____

Why did you decide to purchase this Workbook? *(Tick one box only)*

☐ Have used BPP Workbooks in the past

☐ Recommendation by friend/colleague

☐ Recommendation by a college lecturer

☐ Saw advertising

☐ Other _____

During the past six months do you recall seeing/receiving either of the following?
(Tick as many boxes as are relevant)

☐ Our advertisement in Accounting Technician

☐ Our Publishing Catalogue

Which (if any) aspects of our advertising do you think are useful?
(Tick as many boxes as are relevant)

☐ Prices and publication dates of new editions

☐ Information on Workbook content

☐ Details of our free online offering

☐ None of the above

Your ratings, comments and suggestions would be appreciated on the following areas of this Workbook.

	Very useful	Useful	Not useful
Introductory section	☐	☐	☐
Quality of explanations	☐	☐	☐
How it works	☐	☐	☐
Chapter tasks	☐	☐	☐
Chapter Overviews	☐	☐	☐
Test your learning	☐	☐	☐
Index	☐	☐	☐

	Excellent	Good	Adequate	Poor
Overall opinion of this Workbook	☐	☐	☐	☐

Do you intend to continue using BPP Products? ☐ Yes ☐ No

Please note any further comments and suggestions/errors on the reverse of this page. The Head of Programme for this edition can be emailed at: nisarahmed@bpp.com

Please return to: Nisar Ahmed, AAT Head of Programme, BPP Learning Media Ltd, FREEPOST, London, W12 8AA.

REVIEW FORM (continued)

TELL US WHAT YOU THINK

Please note any further comments and suggestions/errors below.